D
20-4

15882

D0722247

A CLIMBER
IN
THE WEST COUNTRY

by

EDWARD C. PYATT

DAVID & CHARLES
NEWTON ABBOT

7153 4248 7

Printed in Great Britain for David & Charles (Holdings) Limited
by Clarke, Doble & Brendon Limited
Cattedown Plymouth

CONTENTS

LIST OF ILLUSTRATIONS

FIGURES

Photographs not individually acknowledged above are by the author

ACKNOWLEDGEMENTS

I WISH to thank my West Country climbing friends for the help and inspiration which have made this book possible. I have been particularly fortunate in knowing those great exponents of West Country climbing exploration—the late A. W. Andrews, who had been climbing there for years before we collaborated in the first climbers' guidebook to West Penwith; the late C. H. Archer, enthusiastic traverser of the foreshore, and Keith Lawder, who has been with me on most of the exploratory work described here; the book owes much to these three.

For helpful comment and criticism on various chapters I have to thank Cecil Agar, Peter Biven, John Cleare, Keith Lawder, Cyril Manning, Geoffrey Mason and Harry Pearman. Any errors that remain are my own responsibility and arise from ignoring their advice.

Acknowledgement is made to the following for permission to quote from the journals and books listed:
Longmans, Green & Co, Ltd for *Rock Climbing in the British Isles—England* by W. P. Haskett Smith; Robert Hale, Ltd for *The Scilly Isles* by C. C. Vyvyan and *Dartmoor* by E. W. Martin; J. M. Dent & Sons, Ltd for *The Coast Scenery of North Devon* by E. A. N. Arber and *Commando Climber* by M. E. B. Banks; Eyre & Spottiswoode (Publishers), Ltd for *Mountains with a Difference* by G. Winthrop Young; John Murray for *This my Voyage* by Tom Longstaff; John Cleare for an article in the *Alpine Journal*; A. D. M. Cox for an article in *Oxford Mountaineering*; Miss E. Andrews for the works of the late A. W. Andrews; Mrs Archer for the works of the late C. H. Archer; C. Bonington for an article in the *Climbers' Club Journal*; E. W. Shipton for *Upon that Mountain*; Keith Lawder for joint articles in the *Climbers' Club Journal*; the Climbers' Club for their guidebooks; the editors of the *Alpine Journal, the Climbers' Club Journal* and the *Rucksack Club Journal*.

The responsibility for the pictures is recorded in the accompanying notes on the illustrations.

D. Atkinson prepared the figures; E. F. G. McGill provided photographic assistance. The Libraries of the Alpine Club, the Borough of Richmond upon Thames, the Geological Survey, Devon County (Great Torrington Branch), and the Chelsea Speleological Society helped with references and material.

Keith Lawder carried out the huge task of checking all the OS Grid References.

My wife has given tremendous help and encouragement at all stages of the project. Christopher and Gillian have also made their contributions.

EDWARD C. PYATT

Hampton Hill
November 1967

INTRODUCTION

THE climber who visits the West Country at the present time has much to look forward to, yet only a few years before, unless bound for West Penwith, he would hardly have bothered to take along his rope and boots. All is now changed and the range of prospects is wide indeed. Not only is there scope for conventional climbing activities from gentle walking on hill and cliff top to rock ascents of the highest standards, but here also the sport of coasteering was originally cradled and here it has seen its most extensive development.

There are no real mountains in the West Country and thus no mountain rock climbing. There are, however, rock outcrops on the various moors especially on Dartmoor, where the Dewer Stone is the nearest approach in dimensions and quality to a mountain crag. There is limestone climbing of the highest class in Somerset, where the Avon Gorge is the practice climbing ground *par excellence*. Cheddar Gorge, on the other hand, which has some of the finest rock scenery in the country, may well be closed to climbers sooner or later because of the danger of rock falls. Both Dorset and the Torbay area of Devon have the exciting combination of limestone and sea cliffs. There are a few climbable rocks in quarries and away from the hills.

The major coastal climbing areas are the granite cliffs of West Penwith and Lundy, which provide climbs of all standards of difficulty. Development of the Torbay limestone, particularly that on Berry Head, is proceeding so rapidly that this will soon be a major area too and invite comparison with the great crags of Anglesey. Dorset limestone is also of considerable importance, lying as it does within easy weekend range of London. Other rock types in other places also have their adherents, notably the Lizard and the coastline between Bude and Hartland Point. There is a sea level traverse for many miles along the North Devon coast, while any development of chalk climbing which may take place in future years will find ample scope along the coast of Dorset. The major West Country islands—Lundy, Steep Holm and the numer-

11

ous Isles of Scilly—are all of great interest and in addition there is a host of lesser islets and stacks.

Plenty of fine hill walking can be had on distinctive ranges like the Mendips and the Quantocks and rough moorland walking in the wild country of Dartmoor, Exmoor, Bodmin Moor and the other granite masses of Cornwall. Dartmoor and Exmoor are National Parks and supposedly preserved for our enjoyment, though there are grave doubts whether this is at all effective. High Willhays, 2,038 ft, on Dartmoor is the highest point in the west of England. Walks can be devised along ridges and watersheds, often the lines of ancient trackways where the remains of prehistoric man are found in situations which appeal to the hill walker of today. The watershed between the Bristol Channel and the English Channel would make a particularly interesting and unusual line to follow.

The coastline of the West Country is a paradise for the walker. The National Parks Commission has designated more than 500 miles of it—a continuous length from Minehead in Somerset to Studland in Dorset—as a Long Distance Footpath under the National Parks and Access to the Countryside Act, 1949. This is the South-West Peninsula Coast Path, to which I shall refer frequently hereafter, abbreviating the somewhat verbose title to S-W P C Path. Negotiations over rights-of-way are still in progress but eventually the whole of this distance will be free and open to the walker, providing him with a continuous expedition of great length and interest almost entirely along, or very close to, the cliff edge.

The Mendip Hills are one of Britain's major caving areas, while there are lesser caves, still of considerable interest, in South Devon. To realise the tremendous scope which remains for cave exploration one has only to compare the trickle of water flowing in the various caves known at present with the volume which emerges at the base of the hills where the limestone ends.

Much of West Country climbing activity is associated of course with the coastline. Sea and mountains offer a similar type of challenge to mankind and, as Eric Shipton has pointed out, a person of appropriate outlook might easily be turned towards one or the other in his youth by quite casual circumstances:

> Any particular set of tastes can find expression in a variety of ways, and most people who know what they want have a large choice of routes along which they can pursue the same objective. If

at an early age I had been taught to handle and navigate a small boat, I think I should have derived as much satisfaction from sailing as I have from climbing; the sea would have absorbed my interest and enthusiasm in the same way that mountains have done. The two pursuits offer the same opportunities for personal identification with natural phenomena—both demand a thorough knowledge of the elements concerned and skill in dealing with them; both provide an unlimited outlet for physical energy and a capacity for aesthetic enjoyment; both open up a vast field of possibility, each has its own great tradition of adventure, each has its history. . . .

At the coastline the diverse sports of sea and mountain are brought, as it were, face to face and a range of activities combining some of the interesting features of both becomes possible. Coasteering, which may be defined as the application of the principles of mountaineering and rock climbing to the scenic features of the coastline, offers walking on varied terrain, climbing on a variety of rock types, the ascents of virgin summits, novel techniques including complex problems of access and all in novel surroundings. 'Cliff climbing,' says M. E. B. Banks, writing here of Cornwall, 'is not just another sort of mountaineering. It is a completely different, yet parallel, cult with its own distinctive atmosphere and usage.'

It is necessary at this early stage to define with some precision the geographical terms used in descriptions of coastal features (see Fig 1). The line of the abrupt transition between the sea and the land is called a cliff. When the cliff is flat-topped the limit of our area of activity is set by the edge of cultivation; when the top slopes up to the summit of a coastal hill or hill ridge, the so-called hog's back type of cliff, then our area includes all the seaward facing slopes. The shore is a wave-worn platform below the cliff and when covered by rocks or sand is known as a beach. Between high water mark and the cliff is the backshore, while the remainder of the shore between high and low water marks is known as the foreshore. The sea immediately adjacent to the land is known as offshore—the definition of this is loose and depends on the numbers of islands, reefs, etc. The limit of our area of activity in this direction is where the sea becomes relatively unbroken even at low tide. The cliff may rise from the backshore, the foreshore or the offshore and it is in each case correspondingly named. Pinnacles (stacks) and islets on the foreshore and offshore are distinguished largely by their relative bulk—an islet has an area large compared

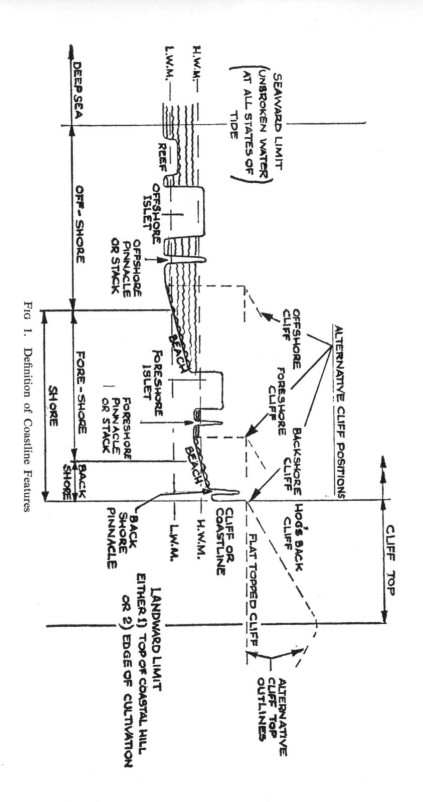

Fig 1. Definition of Coastline Features

with its height, a pinnacle (stack) is by comparison slender. When an offshore islet becomes sufficiently large it is an island and its features are then treated in detail in the same way as those of the mainland. The first essential for access to features on the shore is an easy way down the cliff; these can usually be worked out at intervals even in fairly steep terrain, but in exceptional circumstances there may be no alternative to an approach by sea. The climber can rope down the cliff of course, but then he must be able to climb up again. On the backshore the tide has no effect on the coasteer's mobility; the foreshore on the other hand can only be reached for a limited period on either side of low tide and for the rest of the time foreshore features must be approached by water or, in the case of a continuous cliff, by a traverse from the nearest accessible backshore. Offshore features can only be reached by boat or by swimming, or in the case of cliffs by a traverse from the adjacent foreshore. A headland is a part of the coast, usually upstanding, which protrudes into the sea in advance of the general line of the coast or else marks a turning point in its direction. A promontory is similar but usually narrower, steeper-sided and more rocky. The recesses between headlands when extensive are bays, when on a much smaller scale—coves. A narrow, steep-sided inlet carrying deep water, often called a zawn in Cornwall, marks the removal by the sea of softer rocks from between layers that are harder. Caves are formed similarly in the cliff face by the removal of less resistant material. The same process of attack on the sides of a promontory produces the characteristic arches on rocky coastlines and later these collapse leaving behind pinnacles made of the tougher rocks—the virgin summits of the coasteer.

The sea itself plays three distinct roles in our sport. First, it acts as a barrier permanently denying access (except by boat) to offshore stacks, islets and islands and it complicates access to foreshore features. Secondly it is an additional hazard in the climbing itself, making the rocks either smooth or slimy, covering and uncovering the place the climber has to pass and unsettling him by its movement beneath his feet. Finally the sea is the background to all coasteering activities, often superior to the hill or mountain background of British mountain rock climbing.

We are now in a position to appreciate the full range of coasteering. The cliff top provides a terrain very similar to that of a British mountain ridge, but more diverse. There is walking uphill and downhill as headlands and coves alternate; there are extensive views with plentiful verticals all around. The only access problems are those imposed by man. Cliff top paths exist in many places, a hangover from the days when coastguards carried out regular patrols. There are numerous rights-of-way and in any case the immediate cliff edge is useless land and walking on it does no very great harm. The way can be varied by taking to the rougher going of the beach, where sand, shingle and boulder hopping are complicated by pools, streams, slime- and weed-covered rocks and curtains of harder rock running across. The backshore is straightforward enough, but walking on the foreshore demands careful attention to the tides. The varied shore life, the unravelling of the local geology here exposed to view, the hunt for interesting or valuable shells or pebbles and the sea itself all help to beguile the way.

When there is no backshore and little or no foreshore (that is when high and low water marks are close together horizontally) a traverse from one easy way down to the next may well provide problems of access and of climbing of absorbing difficulty. Perhaps the most usual situation presents backshore and foreshore in the coves and foreshore or even offshore problems at the headlands. There will be points which can only be passed at the lowest tide, or even only at an exceptionally low tide; these have to be reached at the precisely correct time and, once behind, the remainder of the climb must 'go' as it would not be possible to return after the tide had begun to rise. To be cut off in this way would be really dangerous only in rare cases—it is usually possible

———

Cheddar Gorge, Somerset. A. Greenbank uses artificial climbing tactics in the first ascent of Coronation Street above the snow-covered depths of the Gorge

to scale the cliff out of reach of the sea and wait for it to recede once again. These traverses are a unique feature of coasteering.

Sea cliffs themselves can give straightforward rock climbing of a conventional type, complicated by the usual problems of access. However, only certain favoured rock types, granite for example, offer large areas of sound material with buttresses, ribs, cracks, chimneys, etc, similar to mountain rocks. On other formations there are often considerable masses of inferior rock unclimable because of poor quality, shattered nature, steepness, etc, and the usable routes have to be selected with great care. It often happens that the last few feet to the cliff top consist of loose rock or very steep vegetation and it is worthwhile to verify that a route can be finished before embarking on it from below. Rocks near sea level have been rounded off by wave action and all loose material soon gets carried away. Where the foreshore is a wave cut platform of any size at all very little erosion of the cliffs takes place even over a period of several years. Recent cliff falls are easily detected and avoided.

The virgin summit, even the little visited summit, has long since disappeared among home mountains. To do genuine exploration it is necessary to travel very far afield indeed, while the making of a new climbers' route on a mountain crag face in these islands is only possible for the very expert. Coasteering opens up a new field here, providing in the shape of islets, pinnacles and so on, the unclimbed summits which were the original objectives of mountaineering. Numerous possibilities await, each with its own added problem of access. The climbing, too, may be far from straightforward; if the pinnacle is steep and there is reason to

———

Avon Gorge, Somerset. High above the road and the tennis courts, a climber on Lich Gates (HVS) uses artificial methods to assist progress

B

suspect the quality of the rock, new and ingenious tactics may well be called for in the surmounting of it.

Caves, often difficult to discover, let alone to enter, are also plentiful in sea cliffs everywhere and, though having little in common with the limestone solution caves found inland, they provide another worthy field for exploration.

Islands have a charm of their own for the mountain lover, who finds in them the same quality of remoteness and inaccessibility which may once have appealed to him in mountains. This is accentuated if there is rock climbing on the island cliffs and even more if climbing is needed to reach the island at all. In any case the first approach has to be by boat, requiring an expertise of its own in a quite different sport. Generally speaking the island presents all the same features in detail that we have outlined for the mainland above.

The coasteer has all these things for his enjoyment, as well as better weather, more colourful backgrounds, a wider variety of flora and fauna (of the sea as well as of the land) and less gallery for his activities. Moreover, he can combine his sport more readily with the usual family holiday pattern.

The development of coasteering in the West Country has been the work of certain notable pioneers. Tom Longstaff, who later climbed and explored all over the world, began his climbing on the sea cliffs of North Devon in 1887 at the age of twelve. Within five years he and his friends were using a rope and had made traverses from bay to bay on the mainland, as well as climbing on Lundy. Of these early years he later wrote:

> Climbing on sea cliffs does not grant us that freedom of spirit which we find on mountain tops. The surf confines us with elemental restraint; thus far and no farther. Yet it is this very intimacy with the sea's infinite variety of mood which gives to cliff climbing its unique fascination.

Arthur Westlake Andrews, who devoted a lifetime to the enthusiastic promotion of cliff climbing in West Cornwall, was the real father of coasteering. He went first in 1873 at the age of six, but he did not begin serious climbing until after the turn of the century:

> I had climbed and rambled for some ten years in the Alps and the British Isles but till then had never realised the possibilities of what seemed at first glance a rather dull and low coast. I had had the ambition to make a complete traverse of the shore of the

British Isles between high and low tide marks, as far as practicable, but have not yet finished it. We began our pilgrimage with a traverse from St Ives to Pendeen in which, though much was easy, we met unexpected obstacles.

Later in life he turned to poetry; in these few lines he captures the whole essence of the more difficult type of shore traverse:

> Tide coming in too fast and on our left
> A cliff we could not climb and on our right
> Nothing but sea, America and night.

For more than forty years Andrews alone preserved a continuity in coasteering and almost all cliff climbing activities in England were organised by him here in his own territory.

The pioneer of coasteering in North Devon was E. A. N. Arber, whose geological work before World War 1 will be referred to in due course. In his writings he forecast almost exactly the sort of cliff foot traverse that was subsequently carried out, offering at the same time a comparison between this and rock climbing and mountaineering:

> The work of 'beach crawling', as it may be called, has something in common with rock climbing, but it is much less dangerous, for the rocks are less treacherous, and in the case of a slip one can only fall a few feet. The art consists in moving rapidly from one boulder of from five to twelve feet in height to another of similar height and for this purpose long alpenstocks are found to be very useful. It would indeed be a proud accomplishment to have traversed the whole of the shoreline from Porlock to Boscastle. Whoever manages to accomplish this feat in the future will have seen wonders in the way of cliff scenery and can also boast of a remarkable record. After many expeditions with experts in the art of 'beach crawling', there are still several miles which the author has been unable to traverse by means of the beach. One hesitates to say that the task is impossible, for at spring tides one can sometimes accomplish seemingly extraordinary feats in the way of rounding obstinate points. Certainly it will not be perfected without special studies of the difficulties and opportunities, studies as serious, perhaps, as those which were necessary when, in former days, some untrodden Alpine peak was to be attacked.

And further on he added:

> To those who are interested and active no better advice can be given than to combine with the cliff walks the more difficult and much more laborious method of progressing along the beach. . . . It is true that in many districts, in order to make any progress along

the beach, energy, strength and determination are necessary, and a small element of danger is not altogether absent. The latter is never, however, serious, if proper precautions are taken. Rock climbers, and those fond of scrambling in unfrequented places, will find in the beaches of the roughest portion of this coast a new paradise, which is certain to meet with their approval. The 'going' is of the roughest description, and progress is slow, a uniform rate of about a mile an hour being reckoned on average.

C. H. Archer, one time member of the Alpine Club, who had had experience of climbing in the Far East, retired to the West Country early in the 1950s. Without any knowledge of the similar pioneering work by Andrews in West Penwith and with considerable aid from his close friend Cecil Agar, he carried out during the next decade the tremendous shore traverse conceived by Arber. This route from Foreland Point to Saunton Sands is, without doubt, the longest and most sustained piece of exploration in the sport and is a model for similar work on other coastlines as yet untried.

The problems and techniques of coasteering differ in many respects from those of British mountain rock climbing. For example, in appraising the possibilities of a cliff face the coasteer must remember that only a few of the great range of rocks he may encounter will be reasonably usable, while a great many more will not. Granite is a near approach to a mountain rock (in fact it forms mountains in some parts of Britain) and good granite and bad can be fairly easily distinguished from below. It is necessary in other rock types, however, to be very discriminating and, in general, places which look easy will be difficult, while places which look interestingly difficult will most likely be impossible. A route may exist because a line of good rock runs up an area of bad or because the conformation of the cliff produces a line where the problems of the poor quality rock can be tackled and overcome. Steepness and rock quality are in fact inter-related. In general it may be said that routes are few compared with the amount of rock that is exposed. It should be noted too that a real examination of most sea-facing crags can only be carried out from the sea or the shore; the view from the cliff top is necessarily restricted and may well miss essential features hidden below convex slopes. The working out of climbing-ways-down is similarly difficult, though in this case the sea or shore view may be misleading also because of foreshortening.

To solve his access problems the coasteer needs two items of equipment outside the range of normal rock climbing. For offshore work and sea approaches in general a boat must obviously be used, as was done for the ascents of the sea stacks of St Kilda. The actual technique of handling a small boat under these circumstances could be the subject of a book of its own. To land even on very easy rocks demands a relatively calm sea and an experienced crew; this aspect of coasteering can certainly not be lightly embarked upon. If stretches of cliff unsuitable for climbing intervene between the climber and some desirable objective, say a pinnacle on the backshore, the use of a rope ladder is legitimate in order to gain access. A rope or short ladder hung from the cliff top over an otherwise impassable exit to a climb might make a route where it would not otherwise be justifiable. If confident of his ability to get up again, the climber may perhaps descend cliff walls by abseil, but this certainly commits him to the ascent or a laborious return up the rope using Prusik Knots or some modern device for rope gripping. A technique of mountaineering which may have some applications is the so-called Tyrolean traverse, where a rope is projected over the summit of a pinnacle from an adjacent accessible rock mass and fixed on the far side; it is then used as a bridge across the gap, in much the same way as a rope would be used for a river crossing. A rope similarly projected over a pinnacle from the foot can be used to climb it with the aid of some Prusik type device or alternatively as a means of hauling up a light ladder.

Clothing for the sea cliff climber, I once wrote, 'should vary from nothing to as little as possible' and this is certainly the right outlook when the weather warrants it. In a similar vein, Peter Biven, in an account of a climb at Bosigran, once said 'the day was quite tropical, and clothing consisted mainly of pitons and 200 ft of rope'. When climbing in shorts, knee-pads of a style sometimes worn by soccer goalkeepers, or for rugby on very hard grounds, are a useful kit item. The bare back, so pleasant for most of the work, will need covering in rock chimneys or when 'bush whacking' through thickets or thorns. Archer recommended lightweight leather gardening gloves for dealing with underwater acorn barnacles and with cliff top brambles. For the latter he also carried secateurs. Climbers who concentrate on very hard rock climbing will use the footgear to which they are accustomed, but for general use in all branches of the sport the now old-fashioned plimsoll, or tennis shoe, is still hard to beat. This might be combined advantageously with a small two- or four-point crampon, fastened to the sole for very steep vegetation and grass. Vibram soled boots are also suitable for most of the going likely to be encountered. A crash helmet would have its advantages in this sort of terrain. Pitons will be needed, if not for use in a conventional fashion, at least to assist extrication from areas of poor quality rock or in places where all potential belays turn out to be loose. As well as the normal rock pitons, some larger ones suitable for earth, say one-in angle and twelve- to fifteen-ins long, of steel or alloy, should also be included. A slater's pick is a useful tool which can also serve as a piton hammer; the pointed blade is handy for removing vegetation from holds or even as a hold or belay when driven into the earth. A conventional short ice-axe/piton hammer would serve similarly. On the Matterhorn, Edward Whymper used as a climbing aid a short rope and grapnel which he threw up to catch on the rocks above his head; the Commandos practice a similar technique on the cliffs near St Ives. This last is the only record of such a device on sea cliffs but it might possibly be applied, with care, to some of the problems of coasteering.

The basic climbing moves here are identical with those used on mountains, so far as use of holds, disposal of body, simultaneous anchorage at a number of points, etc, are concerned. A novice coasteer can learn a great deal, therefore, from a treatise on the technique of rock climbing. There are some small differences; for example one soon becomes accustomed to moving around on vegetation much steeper than is usual on mountains. Climbing in or near the water has its own problems for falling into the sea can in fact be very dangerous and a rope should always be used when climbing above water except in the easiest places. At some time it may be necessary to take to the water—the local rule in West Cornwall, enunciated by Andrews, was that 'the climber is climbing as long as his nose is above water'. Archer never scrupled about swimming, but he did recommend that the swimmer should always be attached for safety to a companion anchored on the land. To describe the technique of passing among boulders covered with slime or seaweed Andrews used the eloquent expression 'touch-and-pass'; it is impossible to be precise about what it involves. When the sea is rising and falling it may be necessary to cross or climb between waves; periodically there is a wave larger than the rest, traditionally the seventh, though there is in fact no basis for this belief. The tradition that large waves come in pairs is equally fallacious.

Granite is a suitable rock for the novice learning to climb and there are many places where routes of varying shades of difficulty can be tried with a rope from above. It is suitable too for early leading since there are big holds and ledges on the easier climbs and safe belays are usually available. It would be unwise, on the other hand, to take first steps on any of the other coastal rocks. The sort of experience needed to tackle these safely might well be acquired by previous practice on some handy mountain crag. To endure the present-day crowds to this end might well be worthwhile.

It is important to note that the mention hereafter of any crag, cliff, cave, hill walk or shore does not necessarily imply a right to climb or to enter. Most places, even those which may not appear so, are in fact private property. Entry may be by usage, less frequently by right. The traveller, whatever his purpose in the countryside, must behave in a responsible manner and with due deference to the rights of the owners. It is particularly vital to preserve good relations with local people, so that the visits of strangers, even if no longer a pleasure to them, are at least not actively resented.

In conclusion two small textual points require explanation. Standards of climbs are referred to by capital letters as follows— M (moderate), D (difficult), VD (very difficult), MS (mild severe), S (severe), HS (hard severe), VS (very severe), HVS (hard very severe), XS (exceptionally severe)—a conventional shorthand among climbers. All sites mentioned in the book are listed in the index with their Ordnance Survey Grid References; the system is explained on the covers of OS Maps or in a readily available OS publication. There is a glossary of some common climbing terms on page 184.

1

SOMERSET AND BRISTOL

THE Mendip Hills run westwards for twenty miles or so from Frome to Weston-super-Mare. There is a steep scarp slope to the south, especially between Cheddar and Wells above the River Axe. The top is a vast plateau two or three miles wide which slopes down irregularly and less steeply to the north, though there are more precipitous slopes towards the western end. These hills consist of a thick layer of Mountain Limestone resting on Old Red Sandstone; the whole has been sharply folded, so acutely folded in fact that the highest points, Black Down, 1,067 ft, between Cheddar and Burrington, North Hill near Priddy, Pen Hill above Wells and the hills over against Shepton Mallet are actually of sandstone exposed by the erosion of the limestone cover. Water flowing across the surface of these hills disappears below ground at the junction of the sandstone and the limestone, the downward sloping strata of which carry the drainage by underground ways to the valleys. The limestone is honeycombed with these water-worn caves, only a small proportion of which have yet been penetrated by man. The biggest caves on the upper slopes, the 'caves of engulfment', can be descended in many places to 400 to 500 ft below the surface before the passages become too small or too waterlogged; the 'caves of debouchure' at the foot of the hills, where the water reappears, have in some cases been followed for several hundreds of feet before they too become impassable. On the upper surface of the limestone are numerous funnel shaped depressions, called swallet holes, which indicate the presence of caves beneath. These may be former stream entrances, they may be due to solution or again to the collapse of a cave roof. Here is the place to dig for a cave. The work may be profitable as it was at G.B. Cavern or Longwood Swallet, or completely unrewarding as in Waldegrove Swallet—the only way to find out is to try!

Here and there on the escarpment are fine cliffs, notably in the gorges at Cheddar, Ebbor and Burrington, all of which may well have arisen from the collapse and exposure of former large caves. These are the principal climbing areas. Moving westwards towards the sea the hills are lower; Crook Peak (628 ft) of the distinctive outline is followed by Bleadon Hill which looks down on Weston-super-Mare. The line of the hills continues to the sea's edge in the rocky promontory of Brean Down and on into the Channel where the island of Steep Holm, surrounded by limestone cliffs, reaches 256 ft. Facing Brean Down across Weston Bay is the wooded Worlebury Hill topped by Worlebury Camp, a ten-acre fortification with a unique series of circular pits believed to have been used for storage. This was the termination of ancient trackways which came by hill and ridge from Salisbury Plain to the Bristol Channel, passing on the way the great camps of Maesbury near Shepton Mallet and Dolebury above Churchill, as well as many lesser. From here the sea passage was probably made to Wales. Later a Roman road took the same line when the Romans began to work the Mendip lead ores.

With so many things to see—rocks and gorges, caves and swallets, antiquarian remains and relics of former mine workings—there is plenty of scope for the devising of interesting walkers' routes, even though there is no trackway which follows the actual scarp edge. The height and the flatness of the surroundings make for extensive views. From Pen Hill, for instance, the distant view includes Foreland Point, sixty miles away, and the waters of the Bristol Channel, while far away to the south the Golden Cap on the Dorset coast peeps through the gap between Pilsdon Pen and Lewesdon Hill. The planned eruption of a 900 ft TV mast on Pen Hill in the near future will ruin it as a viewpoint, as well as spoiling the view of these hills from the surrounding plain.

North-west of the Mendips, beyond the valley of the River Yeo, Mountain Limestone appears once again on Broadfield Down, notably in the narrow valleys of Brockley Combe and Goblin Combe. North-west again, parallel to the River Severn, a ridge of the same rock runs from Portishead to Clevedon with a fine view over the river to Wales. Enclosed between this and a second ridge east of Clevedon is the valley curiously named Gordano. There is more Mountain Limestone in and around Bristol; extensive faces of this rock are exposed in the Avon Gorge, actually within the City boundary, and these provide what is probably the best rock climbing in the district. There are some small caves also, notably Pen Park Hole in the north by Filton.

The Plain of Somerset, stretching south and south-west from the foot of the Mendips, is bounded on the far side, twenty miles away, by the parallel range of the Quantock Hills. This vast expanse of one-time marshland is broken only by the low ridge of the Polden Hills and by the isolated cones of Glastonbury Tor and Brent Knoll. The Poldens, their whole length traversed by roads, are for the motorised climber. The highest point, 391 ft, is near the southern end; nearby the wooded outlier of Dundon Beacon is surmounted by a camp. Southwards is Sedgemoor where, in the last big battle to be fought in England, the Duke of Monmouth's cause foundered in the deep channel of Bussex Rhine. Four miles beyond is the site of the Island of Athelney, where King Alfred hid from the Danes. This wedge of land between the Rivers Parrett and Tone is overlooked by a church dedicated to St Michael on top of a hill called the Mump. To the north of the Poldens, among the flatlands of the River Brue is Glastonbury—the Avalon of Arthurian legend. Towering above the plain, Glastonbury Tor (521 ft), topped by the tower of yet another church of St Michael, is a worthy viewpoint. Fifteen miles away over against the coast Brent Knoll (457 ft) rises similarly in isolation; here a camp crowns the summit.

The Quantock Hills are Devonian slates, sandstones and limestones—an outlier really of the higher and more extensive Exmoor block further to the west. The main ridge which runs north-west from Taunton to the sea at Quantoxhead is some ten miles long with a scarp slope facing west and gentler slopes broken by wooded combes to the east. The tops are covered with bracken, heather and scrub oak; the red deer runs wild and is hunted. It is walkers' country with a ridge top trackway from end to end crossing Cothelstone Hill, Lydeard Hill, Will's Neck (1,260 ft, the highest point), Thorncombe Hill and Beacon Hill. The motorised climber is only indifferently served by a few narrow roads, though these do take him to the top in places. There are no rocks and just one cave—in a quarry near Holwell.

Below the scarp of the Quantocks is a narrow strip of the Somerset plain which runs from the Vale of Taunton Deane to the coast near Watchet. Beyond rise the Brendon Hills—a block of hill country with a backbone of higher peaks running from east to west. These hills are readily available to the motorist; this ridge is traversed throughout its length by the minor road from Elsworthy to Wheddon Cross, which for some twelve miles never falls below 1,100 ft. Lype Hill, 1,390 ft, the highest point, is less than half a mile from this road. Over to the north towards Dunster is Croydon Hill, 1,255 ft. There are numerous minor roads in all directions but this nevertheless is a quiet, little known countryside of considerable charm. There are no useful rocks.

Most of the Brendon Hills area and of the extensive moorland block of Exmoor, which adjoins to the west beyond the Exe Valley, form the Exmoor National Park of 265 square miles. Exmoor itself is a plateau, average height around 1,400 ft, with smooth green hills and hardly any of the underlying Devonian slates and sandstones exposed at the surface. Camden, with Defoe concurring, noted it as a 'filthy barren ground', but nowadays cultivated fields run up to 1,000 ft, above which is rough hill pasture and open moorland. There are wild ponies and red deer, the latter hunted here also. The highest point is Dunkery Beacon, an isolated higher hill, or monadnack, which reaches 1,705 ft.

The rock climbing prospects are non-existent but there is considerable scope for hill walking. There are numbers of way-marked tracks in the eastern part of the Moor, particulars of which can be obtained from the National Park authorities. The climber will look for long distance routes seeking out the ridge lines of the watersheds, such as that north of the Quarme and Exe Valleys which runs for some twelve miles from Dunkery Beacon, to Chapman Barrows above Parracombe. The summit of Dunkery Beacon, with its large cairn and beacon hearths, is only three quarters of a mile from a motor road and it is often visited. The beacon fires, it is said, could pass on the message from Plymouth to the Malvern Hills. As soon as Dunkery is left behind the rest of this walk is through wild country indeed, never dropping below 1,350 ft all the way and ending just inside the Devon border.

To the north is the country of the Doones, described by R. D. Blackmore in what is undoubtedly *the* local book—*Lorna Doone*. This is full of fine descriptive writing about Exmoor and its people, but the sites are typical rather than actual. The Badgworthy Valley is often identified as the Doone Valley but the actual site is probably the tributary valley from Hoccombe Combe, which is marked on the 1 Inch OS Map. Some of the other side valleys provide further features of the story; John Ridd and Lorna were married in Oare Church, the final show-down between Ridd and Carver Doone took place in the Cloven Rocks Valley near Simonsbath. The last part of the route is over the wild and desolate western moorlands called the Chains. Eleven inches of rain which fell here in twenty-four hours, nine inches of it falling in one storm, caused the severe flooding and devastation in Lynmouth in August, 1952.

The next watershed line is that between the valleys of the Exe and the Barle, giving a possible route, judging from the map, of seventeen miles or so. It is traversed for much of its length, however, by the B2223 road from Dulverton to Simonsbath, which crosses the summit of Winsford Hill, 1,404 ft, and continues at high level to White Cross. Eventually this road turns down leftwards into the valley, but the hill line continues by Red Stone Hill to join the first route at Exe Head, then on over the Chains to Chapman Barrows. Another possible route of twelve miles follows the watershed between the Barle and the Litton from Hawkridge to Withypool Cross, then along the county boundary to Shoulsbarrow Common.

All our National Parks have their troubles; the land which the Act was intended to preserve is eagerly sought and forcibly acquired for a variety of utilitarian purposes. Here on Exmoor the problem lies in the reclamation of marginal hill land. About 1,000 acres of the Moor are lost per annum, a rate which could effect substantial scenic changes within the next half century. Farmers cannot, of course, be expected not to improve their lands, so that, if the nation requires a National Park here with the present form of this countryside, some method of compensating them will have to be found.

The Blackdown Hills along the Devon border mark the southern edge of the Somerset plain. Between Crewkerne and Chard the ridge carries the A30 trunk road, giving the motorised climber extensive views over Somerset to the Bristol Channel and over Dorset to the English Channel. The highest point is the Windwhistle Inn, 732 ft, near which, says the *New British Traveller* (1784) there used to be a constant spring of water never known to fail, until the day of the Lisbon Earthquake when it suddenly sank and has been dry ever since. Chard is poised athwart the water-shed, for Camden tells us:

Chard stands so high, as to have in it a stream of water, that by being turned (as it easily may be) north or south, will run, as is affirmed, either into the Severn, or the South Sea.

These hills are of greensand, a rock familiar in the Weald, while there is chalk at Combe St Nicholas and Cricket St Thomas. Between Chard and Wellington, Staple Hill rises to 1,035 ft; there are numerous minor roads criss-crossing the countryside. Further west, above Wellington a triangular column commemorating the Duke is set on a 800 ft hill with a wide view.

The line of the Cotswolds extends into Somerset in the neigh-bourhood of Bath and hereabouts the oolitic limestone is quarried as the famous Bath Stone. Dundry Hill, 764 ft, four miles south of Bristol, which gives a fine view over this corner of the county, is an outlier of this same rock. The outcrop can be traced on southwards between the limestone of the Mendips and the chalk hills of Wiltshire and so into Dorset. There are two notable hill sites. Just south of the A303 trunk road, on a hill top close to Sparkford, is Cadbury Castle, long believed to be the site of legendary Camelot. Camden, who called it Camalet, described it as 'a steep mountain, of a very difficult ascent, on the top thereof are the plain footsteps of an old decayed Camp.' The area of it is eighteen acres and the fortifications are complex; active investiga-tion continues. The view over the Somerset plain includes many of the county hill groups, while the ridge continues south towards Sherbourne. Close to the same major road some distance further west is Hamdon Hill, 426 ft, where there are large quarries in the oolite and an extensive earthwork with ramparts three miles in circumference.

THE COAST

Somerset has about eighty miles of coastline, but only the stretch from Minehead to County Gate, some twelve miles, is included in the S-W P C path. The remainder is not for the coasteer—extensive mud flats in Bridgwater Bay, large camp, caravan and holiday sites and the atomic power station at Hinkley Point are certainly not suitable alternatives to mountain terrain.

The hog's back cliffs between Portishead and Clevedon are of mountain limestone and old red sandstone, the latter with agates which are sometimes found among the local pebbles. This coast can be traversed by road at high level or by path at low, but the caravans do not improve the view. At Portishead the vertical height between high and low water marks, the tidal range, has an exceptionally high value, exceeding forty ft, which is greater than anywhere else in the world, excepting only the Bay of Fundy in Nova Scotia. It is a resonance phenomenon due to the tidal frequency and the shape and depth of the estuary.

Three coastal hills around Weston-super-Mare are worthy of note—Middle Hope, which has some cliffs and climbs, Worlebury on the edge of the town and Brean Down to the south on the far side of the River Axe. All of these are worth climbing for the view. Worlebury has a camp; Brean Down, which belongs to the National Trust and is a bird sanctuary under the protection of the Royal Society for the Protection of Birds, has an old fort and some climbing also. There are sandy beaches all down the coast from Weston to Burnham.

Off Brean Down is a reef called Howe Rock and beyond that, two and three quarter miles west-south-west of the Down is the island of Steep Holm, half a mile long, a quarter of a mile wide and 256 ft high, a green dome above steep, high cliffs. Some of the cliffs rise from a rocky shelf exposed at low tide. There are pebble beaches on the south and east and a few small caves on the north side; landing is difficult, impossible in bad weather. Slight ruins remain of a priory founded here in the twelfth century and rebuilt in the fourteenth. In the early 1800s a house was built, which subsequently became an inn and a hotel; this is now in ruins also. Several batteries, established on the island in 1867, were manned until 1903; the remains of these, of contemporary barracks and of Second World War occupation are still much in evidence. At the east end is Calf Rock, at the west end concrete steps lead down to a look-out above Rudder Rock which has been pierced by the sea to form several arches. In other places steps lead down to old pill boxes. The island is now a bird sanctuary administered by the Steep Holm Trust which controls all access. Some climbing seems possible, but it is unlikely to be allowed as long as bird preservation remains paramount, as it most certainly should. Flat Holm, three miles away slightly west of north, has a lighthouse and is as its name implies.

Beyond the River Parrett, the mouth of which is deflected northwards by Stert Peninsula and Island, the coast is dominated by Hinkley Point. When this is behind us we can begin to take an interest in the scenery, but there is little to enthuse over on this side of Minehead. At the end of the ridge of the Quantocks the low grey cliffs at Kilve are oil-bearing shales, while further on St Audries Bay has red cliffs and a coast waterfall. Between Watchet, a small port with a shingle beach, and Blue Anchor Bay the cliffs are of a terra-cotta colour veined with alabaster; there are fossils and the remains of a submerged forest, while skeletons of antediluvian creatures have also been found. Within a few miles now is the thriving resort of Minehead (with sandy beach), which marks the beginning of the really interesting coastline and of the S-W P C Path.

Between Minehead and Porlock Bay are four miles of hog's back cliffs reaching 1,013 ft at Selworthy Beacon. North Hill rises above the town and harbour of Minehead, in the words of a guidebook, extant *circa* 1825:

> . . . on that side nearest the town it is extremely steep and rugged. The rocks hang at a prodigious height above the tops of the houses, and seem every moment to threaten them with destruction.

The S-W P C Path climbs out of the town by Culver Cliff to the summit of North Hill and on over Selworthy Beacon, with its camp, to Hurtstone Point. There are numerous straightforward tracks and paths all over these hills but the steep combes leading down to the sea give more difficult going; Grixy Combe near East Myne is said to be the finest of these. Travellers on the Path can go out to Hurtstone Point where there is a large natural arch,

—————

Bear Rock, Hartland Quay. It does not look like a bear from here, but clearly justifies our original name of Victory Pinnacle. The route is on the left hand face, stepping across at the top from the lower to the higher flake. Near at hand, on the right, is the wall of Consolation Pinnacle

Gull Rock, or can follow a right-of-way behind the Point. This is the east headland of Porlock Bay and gets its name from an occasion when the Devil stood here hurling stones across the valley at Porlock Hill. The terrors of this end of these hills also impressed the author of the previous extract:

> ... the sea has hollowed out a number of immense caverns which serve both to re-echo the roaring of the billows, and to increase their fury and violence. The cliffs at the east corner of this point hang over the beach in a manner peculiarly awful and sublime. When the tide retires, the shore exhibits a vast collection of rocky fragments, which have been separated from the cliffs above, and lie scattered, or piled on each other in wild magnificence. The whole of these rocks are intersected with a variety of metallic veins, and crystals of different sorts and hues.

Porlock Weir, the port for Porlock, lies on the west side of the bay beneath the slopes of another great range of hog's back cliffs which stretches on westwards into Devon. The S-W P C Path climbs up along the edge of Yearnor Wood, turns inland to Culbone and then runs west past the farms at Silcombe, Broomstreet (over 1,000 ft now) and Yenworthy to the county boundary at County Gate. Culbone has the smallest complete parish church in England, only thirty-five ft long and twelve ft four in wide. All along this section of the coast there is a foreshore of boulders, so that there are no real traversing problems for the coasteer; the seaward slopes of the cliffs are wooded almost down to the shore and are, says Archer, 'monotonous except for an occasional fine waterfall'. County Gate, which formerly marked the boundary between Wessex and Devonia, is at 1,059 ft on the main road from Porlock to Lynmouth, which here runs along the summit ridge of the hog's

---

The North Devon Coast. The headlands in the lower left corner are Duty Point and Crock Point; beyond can be seen the small flat area surrounded by woods at Woody Bay. The Bay is bounded on the far side by Wringapeak; the coast between here and the most forward point of the cliffs, Highveer Point close to Heddon's Mouth, is one of the outstanding parts of the shore traverse and includes such features as Big Bluff, Double Bluff and Great Bastion. Further along the coast the typical hog's back cliffs can be seen below the summits of Trentishoe and Holdstone Downs, Great Hangman and Little Hangman. In the far distance the cliffs by Watermouth

back. Below it the private valley of Glenthorne runs steeply down to the sea and a tiny beach in less than half a mile.

CLIMBING

W. P. Haskett Smith, the founder of British rock climbing, made the earliest mention of climbing in Somerset in his *Rock Climbing in the British Isles—England,* written in 1894:

> Somersetshire has little to attract the mountaineer, except the very remarkable limestone scenery on the south side of the Mendips at Cheddar, Ebber and Wookey. There are magnificent cliffs and pinnacles, especially at the first named place, but not many bits of satisfactory climbing. The cliffs are rotten at one point, unclimbably vertical at another, and perhaps at a third the climber is pestered by clouds of angry jackdaws. Ebber Rocks are rather more broken, but on the whole the climbing is not worth much at either place, though the scenery both above ground and below it is such as no one ought to miss.

His attitude is curiously modern for, while his contemporaries were concentrating on mountain crags, he was already thinking in terms of rocks all over the country. At that time, the standards of climbable rock, the quality of material and the nature of the routes were set by the crags of North Wales and the Lake District, while practice rocks were typified by the gritstone edges of the Peak District. Mountain (or carboniferous) limestone, as is found in Somerset, when considered from this viewpoint did not fulfil the basic requirements. It was too steep and appeared superficially to be unreliable; this impression reinforced by the known solubility in the carbonic acid of rainwater; the crags were not on the flanks of mountains, and were in most cases too high to provide the practice with a top rope which makes lesser rocks so useful as training grounds. The attitude just after the turn of the century was summarised by Ernest Baker, a notable climber, though not of the first rank, who was ultimately converted to caving and played a prominent part in the exploration of the caves of Mendip. In *Nether World of Mendip,* written in collaboration with H. E. Balch in 1907, he wrote of Cheddar Gorge:

> Two furlongs above its entrance the ravine makes a double curve like a gigantic figure three. The two crescents of beetling limestone, with their jutting horns, that appear to the astonished beholder underneath like towering pyramids and slim aiguilles, rise to a

vertical height of 430 ft, and, being absolutely unassailable, they fill a crag climber's mind with admiration tempered by regret. What enhances their grandeur, while it softens the savage aspect of the sheer and ledgeless precipice, is the bountiful vegetation clinging wherever it can find a hold, dark shrouds of ivy and darker masses of yew standing out against the grey rock in beautiful relief. Would the indomitable scramblers who haunt Lakeland at Easter, we asked ourselves, have forced a way up these tremendous 'chimneys' if the Cheddar cliffs had been pitched somewhere in the latitude of Wastdale? We went so far as to reconnoitre one alluring fissure, 200 ft or more in length, but the gap between its base and the first feasible lodgment was insuperable.

It is interesting to note, however, that at this same time Mountain limestone in Derbyshire was already receiving attention at the hands and feet of those pioneer climbers, James Puttrell and Henry Bishop. The latter writing in the *Climbers' Club Journal* in 1910 shows none of the inhibitions which bedevilled Baker:

> It has been urged against Mountain limestone that its treacherous nature unfits it for the climber's attention. But the few who have really studied its idiosyncrasies, and who have learnt to treat it with deserved respect, will retort that it offers absolutely the finest training in the art of deciding, by observation and actual test, as to the stability or otherwise of each apparent hold. They will have found that the larger pieces are often less reliable than the small projections; that nails will 'bite' to a very slight extent only; and that the weight can sometimes be advantageously distributed over six or even more points. Frost is occasionally a useful agent in binding together small fragments. The practical value of a training on limestone will be apparent when dealing with doubtful rocks on our own mountains, especially on new, 'unswept' climbs; a much greater degree of safety is possible to the 'limestoner' than to the man accustomed only to absolutely firm material.

These sentiments sound very reasonable and modern to us today though at that time most weighty opinion was on the other side.

Change came but slowly and it was not until 1925 that M. W. Guinness of the Climbers' Club took a serious look at the possibilities in Cheddar Gorge. The great main walls were pronounced unclimbable but above them on the south side the explorers found a second tier of crags which gave some interesting sport. 'These cliffs', he wrote afterwards, 'were of no great elevation and bore a close resemblance to the average gritstone edge. Pleasant climbing was enjoyed, though most routes were made with a rope from above in accepted outcrop tradition.' The great walls did not survive much longer. Four years later W. K. Marples and R. Bates made some long routes on the south side of the Gorge—one at least, Knight's Climb, almost the full height of the wall. Other climbs were made above the covered reservoir higher up the road and on various low rocks on the north side. The very steep crags in the Pinnacle Bay were noted—'more exposed than Holly Tree Wall on Idwal Slabs'—but not climbed. In the early 1930s F. G. Balcombe, an expert climber who later turned to caving and finally to cave diving, began to climb at Churchill and in Avon Gorge. Things were at last gathering momentum. After the War the University of Bristol Mountaineering Club produced a guide-book to the various Somerset rocks. The latest edition of this—Limestone Climbs in South-West England—appeared in 1964. We will now look at the crags in a little more detail.

Looking from Cheddar Village towards the Gorge the view now is much the same as that described in the New British Traveller in 1784—'a stupendous chasm, quite through the body of the adjacent mountains. It appears as if the hill had been split asunder by some dreadful convulsion of nature.' That we no longer find it so awe-inspiring can be put down to our vastly greater experience of travel and scenery. It can be very crowded, though there are places above the cliffs on either side where comparative quiet can still be found.

On leaving Cheddar Village, first Cox's Cave, then Gough's Cave are passed on the right. 300 yds further, a short isolated buttress, the Wind Rock, rising on the south side of the Gorge adjacent to the road, gives a few short climbs. Knight's Climb, the first long route to be done in the Gorge, is just beyond Wind Rock and gives 350 ft of D standard climbing. Fifty yds further on is a quarry on the north side and opposite this is Sceptre, first climbed by H. Banner in 1953, a fine route of VS standard also around 350 ft. The wall on the left of the upper section, which came to be called the Great Wall, or California Wall, was until recently the 'last great unclimbed problem' at Cheddar. An ascent of this, involving climbing of very high standard, was made under the eye of TWW television cameras early in 1965, the climb was called in consequence—Coronation Street. It had been done previously, of course, to ensure that the show would be a success. Further left still is another long route with all pitches artificial. This, at about 430 ft, is the highest crag face in the West Country.

400 yds further up the Gorge is the Horseshoe Bend and another series of long hard climbs. The first two in this area were pioneered by G. West of the Manchester Gritstone Club in 1959, others have followed at regular intervals. Hereabouts is the Pinnacle Bay, which so impressed Baker and the other early climbing visitors, and beyond it an easy gully, the Shoot; this is not a climb but it gives access higher up to a traverse across the upper part of Pinnacle Bay, above which some climbs of 100 ft or so have been made to the top of the cliff. Finally, above the covered reservoir we reach the last group of climbs; two straight-forward routes in the lower section lead to a variety of short rock walls higher up, with several climbs of fairly easy standards.

The striking difference between the two sides of the Gorge is due to rock structure. The limestone beds dip towards the south, so that the crags on the south side, produced by rock falls along joint planes, are nearly vertical. The north side of the Gorge, on the other hand, lies at an easier angle indicating the slope of the bedding planes and the crags are mainly short walls giving single- or two-pitch climbs of forty to eighty ft. Opposite Wind Rock are three such walls one above the other—Five B Wall, Middle Tier and Heart Leaf Bluff. There are others both up and down—a complex topography. The westermost buttress on this side is the Lion Rock, prominently in view from the village.

The Gorge is extremely important as a place of pilgrimage for holiday makers, a great many of whom traverse the road and park their cars in the numerous places provided. Many of the crags are close enough to the road to menace these crowds at all popular times and it seems only sensible, therefore, to climb there outside the holiday season. On the other hand the climber who likes to perform in front of an audience will find this perhaps the finest amphitheatre in the country. New routes of the highest standards are added to the tally every year, so that this is indeed one of the outstanding climbing centres of the West.

A small steep outcrop in the Ebbor Gorge, on the left of the path just after the gorge splays out, gave half a dozen climbs of thirty to seventy ft early in the 1950s. There do not seem to have been any further developments—indeed there is probably no room for any.

Beside the Bristol to Axbridge road just south of Churchill are Churchill Rocks, a sheet of slabs, with steep walls below on the left and above on the right—a miniature, in fact, of Idwal Slabs in North Wales, currently covered with painted slogans. Climbing was first done here in the 1930s by F. G. Balcombe; the best routes, mostly around 100 ft long, are on the right wall and on the left hand side of the slabs, but there are hardly enough of them to make a full day's climbing. Two hundred yards on towards Axbridge there is another outcrop with a route or two.

The steep south side of the Brean Down promontory yielded around forty short climbs (of 20 to 100 ft) in 1958-59; a small typescript guidebook appeared soon afterwards. The best climbing is at the western end close to the abandoned barracks; the eastern end looks down on the beach at Brean, on large numbers of caravans and, in season, holiday makers; the base is accessible except within two hours of high tide. The rock is said to be similar to that of Cheddar; it is sound low down where it is washed by the sea, but the upper parts are very loose. There are climbs on the north face also, while Axe Quarry at the eastern end is accessible at all states of the tide. Swallow Cliff, on the north side of Middle Hope, beyond Weston Bay, also gives a few climbs of thirty to forty ft.

The crags in the Avon Gorge are unique in Britain. Edinburgh and Sheffield come to mind as places with climbing rocks within the City boundary, but only in Bristol is there a crag of mountain magnitude offering long routes up to the very highest standards. Camden draws attention to an unusual feature of the Gorge, which explains perhaps what the climbers are really seeking:

> Where the Avon passes from hence, are high rocks on both sides of the river, as if Nature had industriously contrived them. One of these, which hangs over the river on the east side, is called St Vincent's, and is so stocked with diamonds, that one may gather whole bushels of them. Nothing but the great plenty lessens their value among us, for besides that in transparency they even vie with those from the Indies, they do not yield to them in any other respect, save hardness, but their being smoothed by Nature into six or four corners, does, in my mind, render them more admirable. . . . The other rock on the west bank is likewise full of Diamonds, which by a wonderful contrivance of Nature are contained in hollow reddish flints (for the ground there is red) as if these were big with young.

The *Guide to Watering Places* in 1825 has, probably, the first mention of climbing:

The workmen in the quarries descend the precipices by means of ropes, but, even with the best precautions, they sometimes meet with accidents. . . . Fossilist and botanist should beware of the numberless smooth and tempting paths among the rocks; as a single false step may precipitate the careless adventurer down a hundred yards of perpendicular descent.

Strictures which the present day climber would do well to note carefully.

The climbers' crags are above the Portway on the north bank of the river and stretch about half a mile downstream from Brunel's suspension bridge. The rocks on the other bank have not received the same detailed exploration, partly because, says one writer, they are more difficult of access, 'an extra fifteen minutes' walk'. Supporting the bridge is Suspension Bridge Buttress with six extremely hard routes. There now follows a wide, vegetation filled gully with a red wall of poor rock at the back. The next section of crag, known as Amphitheatre Cliffs, is bounded on the right by Giant's Cave Buttress with one HS climb of 300 ft, and on the left by Battleship Buttress. Here there are a number of routes which start from and in some cases overlook the road; these include Fickle Finger of Fate—the first artificial climb in the Gorge. Between these limiting buttresses the crag is divided into Upper and Lower Amphitheatre Walls by a wide ledge; the lower has several routes, mostly about S standard and a 500 ft girdle traverse; the rock on the upper wall is of poor quality.

The main climbing area is a quarter of a mile further north, above and to the right of the public tennis courts. First comes South Buttress and South Gully followed by Central Buttress and Central Gully, then North Buttress and, finally, immediately behind the tennis courts, Main Wall. South Buttress is of little interest except on the side overlooking South Gully. Here in the lower part is the smooth Fir Tree Slab, said to have been climbed by its easiest routes by local school children years ago. Some of the more recent routes, and there are now around a dozen, may well be beyond them. The Slab is terminated on the right by Bulging Wall (with one climb), while the Sewer Wall, with several fifty ft routes is above on the other side. The South Gully itself gives a climb of M standard.

The Central Buttress, next on the left, is a more serious undertaking. There are half a dozen long climbs of around 200 ft of HS or VS standard. The Piton Route is notable as one of the earliest climbs in the Gorge, pioneered by F. G. Balcombe in 1936. Central Buttress is a popular climb, much photographed. Exhibition Slab, on the lower right of this buttress, has easy rocks at the foot leading to a selection of single pitch finishes which are steep and hard. Central Gully gives a 200 ft climb of S standard. Behind the tennis courts Morning Slab forms the lower part of the North Buttress; above on the right is Lunchtime Ledge having a big overhang above on the left. Evening Wall rises above the ledge. Except for the extreme right, the routes on Morning Slab are of high standard and there is a 440 ft girdle traverse. Evening Wall routes average 100 ft with a range of standards. A route of D standard, The Arête, can in fact be taken from base to summit here so that even the moderate climber can enjoy the scenery.

The next crag is the famous Main Wall which, with a line of overhangs, is as impressive, says C. J. S. Bonington, as the East Buttress of Clogwyn du'r Arddu. He it was who led the exploration of this crag during the 1950s, when the routes curiously named Maltravers, Malpractice, Malbogies, Mercavity and Bon Bogies were done. Here is his description of one of them:

So far the route had given little trouble; but we were to be disillusioned. To avoid an untrustworthy overhanging block, it was necessary to step down to the foot of a groove and then bridge up it, using for the right foot a series of loose flakes, until it was possible to pull across to a break in a rib farther left. The only hold I could now find was a horizontal crack at chest height. I stayed there some time, wondering how on earth to get any higher. Finally I knocked in a piton to bolster failing confidence, and made an almost acrobatic move, right foot in the crack alongside my hand, retaining precarious pressure on the wall with my left; I then reached with the other hand to grasp a tree root at full stretch. The position was not much improved. Above a slight overhang was a wall, steep and holdless, clad in ivy. Only to the left was a faint line of weakness. The footholds were quite good for a traverse, but there was little for the hands and the rock was vertical. I made a difficult bridging movement, and balancing over to the left, clawed for some kind of hold amongst the ivy while a shower of earth cascaded about my head. At last I found an unconvincing little rib of rock for my right hand and a moderately firm root for the other. I had to pull up on these, for I knew I could never reverse the last few moves. A pull, a step up, and I was standing on a small grassy ledge. I knocked in a piton and brought Mike up. Meanwhile the ledge collapsed, leaving me suspended from my peg, praying that it was secure. The last pitch gave unpleasant but easy climbing through steep jungle. It had been a most enjoyable and exacting climb.

During the present decade the attack has been intensified and there are now around twenty-five routes, all of superlatively high standard, and two girdle traverses. Malpractice and Depravity, both VS, are the easiest of these. A few hundred yards on are the Sea Walls comprising Black Rock Quarry, Unknown Buttress and Unknown Gully; standards here are very high also. On the Somerset bank of the Avon there is a towpath which gives access to two quarries—Slab Quarry opposite Main Wall with two climbs and Arête Quarry, just beyond Sea Walls, with one.

The advantage of Avon Gorge is its accessibility, yet for the same reason it will appear too public for many a climber's taste. The early morning is a good time for a visit though it may be cold then; 8 p.m. on a summer evening is recommended as an alternative, 'warm rock and the shadows chasing you up the cliff.' The crags, impressively high and steep, would hold their own against most mountain crags or sea cliffs and give a very worthwhile climbing experience. Bonington sums it up:

> When planning a trip to Wales one November week-end, why not come to Bristol instead? The mountains are sure to be cold and wet, the Three Cliffs greasy and Cloggy quite unapproachable. But you will find the rock of the Avon Gorge clean and dry, with all the amenities of civilisation waiting round the corner.

So high are the standards of climbing here now that a specialised guidebook—*Extremely Severe in Avon Gorge*—was produced in 1967. This is for super-experts only, as it is confined to forty or fifty routes of HVS standard and above and ignores everything easier. The author, E. Ward Drummond, introduces a new system for the classification of climbing difficulty which may well find wider acceptance in the future, as well as claiming that the best routes here are more difficult than the hardest in Wales. It will be interesting to see whether others agree with him, though the number that can make practical comparison at this level of achievement is strictly limited.

There are a number of quarries in the Bristol area which give, or would appear likely to give, interesting climbing. There are half a dozen climbs of 100 ft and a few shorter in Uphill Quarry opposite the end of Brean Down. Callow Rocks near the Shipham to Cheddar road have also been used but climbing is not encouraged. There are prospects also, it is said, in two quarries near Weston in Gordano, in two at Backwell, at North Quarry on Crook Peak, Sandford Quarry, Underwood and Dulcote Quarries near Wells and Windsor Quarry near Shepton Mallet. There may well be others too, round and about.

THE CAVES

The Mendip ridge is one of the major caving areas of England. The latest guidebook lists around 175 sites, including caves of engulfment and debouchure, caves vertical and horizontal and all stages between, caves entered by digs or just by following the water, caves in quarries, antiquarian caves, caves for divers and so on. This sport, which has attracted its own big band of enthusiasts, provides an entertaining sideline for the rock climber, who should on no account miss some of this underground climbing experience. To people of only average competence in climbing it can still offer something which has long since disappeared from British mountain crags—the chance of real exploration. You just need to be lucky with your dig! Perhaps the crowning experience in caving is to follow the water through the hill from engulfment to debouchure, as Chevalier has done in France. This has not happened so far in the West Country and geological considerations make it unlikely, nevertheless, untold miles of cave passage still await discovery hereabouts.

The show caves at Cheddar provide a splendid opportunity for the general public to see, brightly illuminated, the wonders of the world below ground. Cox's Cave, discovered in 1837, is the smaller; Gough's Cave, first entered in 1893, has 800 ft of passages on show and plenty more beside. Both are by the roadside on the way to the Gorge.

The third great show cave of Wookey Hole near Wells, the source of the River Axe, has a history going back to earliest times, having been referred to (probably) in the writings of Clement of Alexandria in the 3rd Century AD. William of Worcester, who visited the cave in 1470, wrote—'The hall is about as large as Westminster Hall, and there hangs from the vaulted roof wonderful pendula of stone'. Camden, whose coverage of Britain was remarkably thorough, could not miss such a wonder:

In these Hills, there is a cave of vast winding length, wherein are discovered some wells and rivulets. Ochiehole is the name of it. . . . From a very narrow entrance, it opens into a large vault, the roof whereof (either by reason of its height, or the thickness of the air) they who go in, cannot discover by the light of the candles which they carry with them. After having clambered over several rough and unequal passages among the moist rocks, you come at last to a stream of very clear cold water; which did, in all likelyhood, heretofore discharge itself by the mouth of the cave that now is; but, changing its course, and breaking out by an undercurrent, was the cause that the Cave, of consequence, came to be as we now see it. In several places of this Cave, one may perceive that the droppings of water increase the rock, and are turned into stone; in some places hanging down like icicles.

Various Mendip caves have been a fruitful source of antiquarian remains and museums near and far have been enriched by bones of people and of animals of a byegone age, utensils and other relics of the times when the caves were used for dwelling or for shelter. One of the earliest investigators was the Rev William Buckland who, around 1820, found fifty Stone Age skeletons in Aveline's Hole in Burrington Combe. A few years later remains of bear, lion, woolly rhinoceros, bison, mammoth and many other species were found in the so-called Bone Cave at Banwell. Sir William Boyd Dawkins, who carried out a productive excavation of the Hyena Den at Wookey in the 1850s, was followed by H. E. Balch whose interests extended beyond archaeology to all aspects of caves and who was the real founder of the sport of caving in Somerset. The antiquarian interest has been maintained right up to the present day and this more gentle sort of digging might well attract the cave explorer when he no longer feels capable of the strenuous efforts needed in the search for new caves.

Wookey Hole was the first cave where serious diving was carried out to further the exploration. The inspiration came from F. G. Balcombe following his successful attack on the sump in Swildon's Hole. At the beginning air line suits were used but these were replaced after the Second World War by frogman-type outfits. Beyond the first three chambers, which are open to the public, the divers have now penetrated some 850 ft, as far as an eighteenth chamber.

Another cave which has been known for a very long time is Pen Park Hole, actually inside Bristol boundaries. An early descent was made in 1669 by a Captain Sturmey, accompanied by a 'Mine

Man.' The latter going on ahead in the lower regions was 'uffrighted by the sight of an Evil Spiret, which we cannot persuade him but he saw and for that Reason will go hither no more.'

'Five days after his return,' says a later historian, 'Captain Sturmey was troubled with an unusual and violent Head-Ache, which he imputed to his being in that Vault and falling from his Head-Ache into a Fever, he soon after died.' In 1682 another captain named Collins made a successful descent and found the depth to be fifty-nine, the length seventy-one and the breadth of the cave forty-five yds. After a fatal fall in 1775 the entrance was blocked and it was not until 1956-57 that a new way in was dug by cavers. Access is no longer available.

Lamb Leer near Gibbet's Brow on Mendip top was also an early discovery; miners broke into the large chamber—a 100 ft cube—during the 17th century. Subsequently the entrance fell in and the cave was lost until 1880, when after a search it was rediscovered almost by chance. After another fifty years of neglect the entrance was finally put in order in the 1930s.

Swildon's Hole, close by the church at Priddy Green, was the first really big cave of engulfment to be entered on Mendip top, when H. E. Balch and his friends penetrated some 170 yds as far as the top of a forty ft waterfall in 1901. Soon E. A. Baker joined in. For a time entrance to the cave was forbidden by the owner and the cavers had to resort to the 'new crime of cave burglary'—approaching the cave by night carefully avoiding the keepers and only unpacking tackle and cave clothes when safely inside. They still managed to get in even after a locked grating was fitted across the entrance. Baker describes the sort of world that these early explorers found below ground:

> At the portal a great hollow corbel of stalactite stood out from the wall, like an enormous stoup, its huge rims curved over like the petals of a flower. It stood there in solitary grandeur, but it was a token of transcendent glories beyond. A few more steps, and we saw that we were on the threshold of a fane more beautiful than any made with hands. The rocks to right and left were sheeted with crystalline enamel, its surface powdered thickly with a minute splash deposit, so frail that it gave one a twinge to crush the lovely efflorescence as we moved. One could not go a step without destroying hundreds of these delicate spicules, the work of untold ages of water action. More great corbels stood out from the walls as we advanced; they were richly moulded with concentric rings of stalag-

mite, and these again were carved and chased with wonderful reliefs. From the corbels sprang huge pillars right to the roof, pillars forty ft in height; and from their capitals shining curtains hung down in ample folds, heavy as Parian marble, and as lovely in hue.

In 1914 Baker and E. E. Roberts, a noted Yorkshire speleologist, passed the waterfall but were stopped some distance further on. Exploration was held up by the First World War but in July 1921, Baker alone reached a point over 300 yds from the waterfall. A week or two later a large party of local cavers continued to the end of the cave, nearly 500 ft below the entrance and some 650 horizontal yds from it, the famous sump where the stream runs away under a submerged archway. This was the end until 1936 when F. G. Balcombe and J. Sheppard, using home-made diving equipment, passed the sump and continued a further 200 yds to a second sump. The first cave became Swildons 1, the portion between the sumps, Swildons 2. Considerable exploration has taken place in post-War years. The second sump was passed with proper diving equipment in 1954 and Swildons 3 entered; the diving exploration was extended in 1960 through another sump to Swildons 4, though this had already been reached three years previously by an entirely new route from Swildons 1, which, though it missed out all the sumps, was not without difficulties of its own. Swildons 5 and 6 were explored by divers in 1958 and Swildons 7 and 8 in 1962. Development continued apace, and by 1967 Swildons 12 had been reached. This cave, with over four miles of passages, is now the most extensive in the district and in fact one of the deepest in the country. The following description of the recently discovered Hairy Passage should be contrasted with Baker's lyrical prose above. As in climbing, so also are things below ground much tougher these days:

> This mud duck is passed by going head first on one's left side, so as to get round the bend. The return journey is also head first but on one's right hand side. Care must be taken that one does not build up a flood of water in front of oneself, this especially applies to the large caver, who may well have difficulty in extracting himself from this very claustrophobic mud wallow.

In 1902 Balch forced an entry into the great Eastwater Swallet, three quarters of a mile east of Priddy, and the bottom 420 ft below the surface was reached within the next year or so. Though this cavern has its tough places and its interesting places, there has been no extensive development comparable with that at Swildon's Hole. Altogether there are 3,500 ft of passages, with the normal route of descent involving two ladder pitches. After this no really large cave was entered until 1939, when a dig by F. Goddard and C. Barker in a swallet near Tynings Farm, Charterhouse, gave access to one of the finest caves on Mendip, called G.B. after its discoverers. The main chamber here is 60 ft wide, 200 ft long and 120 ft high; there are nearly a mile of passages and the deepest point is 430 ft below the surface. The original approach route to the main chamber used to be of considerable interest—in one place the caver had to crawl through an S-bend with water on the floor, emerging immediately afterwards head first through a hole and finding himself at the top of an iron ladder in a small pothole; the contortions required to get the feet on to the ladder in these circumstances were often entertaining to watch. Subsequently a much shorter route was discovered. Years of active excavation in various parts of the cave culminated in 1966 in the discovery of an extension beyond the previous farthest point leading to another large chamber, bigger than the Main Chamber in plan though only forty ft high.

In 1944, yet another dig succeeded in reaching a great cave system. This was in the Longwood Valley close to the upper reaches of Cheddar Gorge. Longwood Swallet has 1,000 ft of passages and reaches a depth of 350 ft. The following year a subsidiary series, known as August Hole, branching off from the other, was opened up and proved to be even more extensive— length 3,500 ft and depth 465 ft. 1947 saw some startling developments in a cave which had already been known for some years— Stoke Lane Slocker in the eastern Mendips near Shepton Mallet. A tortuous crawl, previously unnoticed, led off the known cave to a sump and later in the year the sump was free-dived to reach Stoke Lane 2, an extensive system. In 1962 Stoke Lane 3 and 4 were entered using diving equipment and by 1965 explorers had reached Stoke Lane 8; the cave now has over half a mile of passages. Nearby, in Fairy Quarry, a number of caves have been exposed during quarrying operations, the continuation of which is now destroying them. They include Hillier's Cave (1954) with half a mile of passages, Balch Cave (1961) with a third of a mile and Fernhill Cave and Duck's Pot (both 1960), shorter.

Perhaps the most exciting discovery of post-War years took

place at St Cuthbert's Swallet, near Priddy, where another dig broke through into a major cave. Exploration has continued and this is now rated as the most complicated on Mendip, having over one and a half miles of passages and a depth of 400 ft. It is steeper than most other local caves starting with 150 ft, almost vertical, approached by a vertical squeeze near the surface. Because of the complexity and the need to preserve the interior access is closely controlled.

The reasonably competent rock climber capable, say, of leading climbs of VD or MS (climbing) standards should have no difficulty with a straightforward caving expedition of, say, VD (caving) standard. He must learn from a book on technique how to climb a rope ladder and manipulate a safety rope, otherwise the sport demands normal climbing competence under wet conditions allied with a substantial amount of common sense. Some of the various caves at Burrington, notably Read's Cavern, Rod's Pot and Goatchurch Cavern would provide suitable objectives for a first visit. I have visited caves on a number of occasions with parties of climbers and we had no trouble with expeditions like the normal routes in Swildon's Hole, Eastwater Cavern and G.B. Cavern. We often, in fact, descended the cave at night, for sun-bathing during the day overcomes one of the major objections to caving—that one misses out on sunshine. Trips in caves of a higher (caving) standard would benefit from experienced companions and do, of course, demand considerable endurance—unlike most climbing, it is uphill on the way home and energy must be conserved to get back to the surface after a protracted stay below ground. With the great increase in interest in caving during recent years it has become necessary to control access to all major caves and many minor also. This goes a long way towards ensuring that expeditions are only undertaken by those really competent to carry them out and that the interiors are preserved for future generations.

2

NORTH DEVON

THE HILLS

THIS chapter will deal with that part of Devon which lies north of the line Exeter—Okehampton—Launceston A30 trunk road, and is bounded on the east and the west by the Rivers Exe and Tamar. North and east of Barnstaple the rocks are devonian, the remainder of the area consists of shales and sandstones of the carboniferous, the so-called Culm Measures. The highest hills are points on the edge of Exmoor, like Five Barrows, 1,618 ft, which fall fortuitously on the Devon side of the border. The fine line of hog's back cliffs between Lynmouth and Combe Martin reaches 1,145 ft at Holdstone Down with Trentishoe Down and Great Hangman only a few feet lower. There are no other outstanding hills. Though there are many points rising 800 to 1,000 ft, roads and cultivation are often carried over the tops leaving very little room for the hill walker. For example, Bratton Down, 1,079 ft, near Bratton Fleming has a road, B3226, across its summit; the same road in fact traverses several miles of hills at around this level. Others can be picked out on the One Inch map. Two view-points perhaps worthy of mention are Cadbury Hill, 828 ft, with a camp, close to the

———

(above) Scrattling Crack, Baggy Point. A climber descends this long crack in a slab, pioneered more than half a century ago by Tom Longstaff. This, in fact, shows us rediscovering his route in 1962; (below) The Horn of Plenty, near Bude. Covered all over with magnificent holds, this gives a steep but straightforward climb

Tiverton-Crediton road, and Codden Hill, 629 ft, which shows very close contours above Bishop's Tawton.

The watershed between the English and Bristol Channels makes a remarkably sinuous traverse of this part of the county. The limiting rivers rise in the north—the Exe on Exmoor and the Tamar on the hills behind Morwenstow—and reach the sea in the south at Exmouth and Plymouth respectively. Between them the Taw which rises on Dartmoor and the Torridge which starts close to the Tamar terminate in a common estuary in the north. The source of the Torridge is only a dozen miles from its mouth, yet in between it follows an unusually circuitous course far to the south. The main watershed crosses the Somerset border at Wood Barrow, then runs south and south-east, close to the county boundary, nearly to Dulverton. It now turns south across Rackenford Moor, then south-west to Copplestone and by South Zeal over Cawsand Beacon on to Dartmoor. Round Taw Head and by Cranmere Pool, Great Kneeset, Kitty Tor and Sourton Tors, it runs north off the Moor for a few miles, then follows the B3216 road nearly to Holsworthy; now north again by Holsworthy Beacon and the hills west of Bradworthy to enter Cornwall near the A39 trunk road. A very interesting expedition could be made by minor road, by trackway and footpath and sometimes across country along the eighty miles of hill and ridge which form this watershed —a mountaineer's route through the heart of the North Devon countryside. A bridleway connecting Exmoor with Dartmoor with rights-of-way over the whole distance, which is in the course of being worked out, will provide in due course a splendid addition to the walker's amenities in the county.

The Constable, Lundy. First recorded ascent by R. Shaw and J. Logan in 1961. Beyond rises the North Lighthouse

D

THE COAST

Four notable travellers have passed ahead of us along this coast and have left records of their journeys. J. L. W. Page, whose book *The Coast of Devon and Lundy Island* appeared in 1895, was interested in people as well as in places and he deals more with personalities than with the exploration of the recesses of the cliffs. C. G. Harper, a prolific writer on topography, gave us *The North Devon Coast* in 1908, and E. A. N. Arber, a palaeobotanist, his scholarly interpretation of the local geology and geomorphology in *The Coast Scenery of North Devon* of 1911. Finally S. H. Burton's *The North Devon Coast*, 1953, gives a modern view. All four share a common belief in the impossibility of descending to the shore at any point, apart from Heddon's Mouth, between Woody Bay and the Rawns near Combe Martin; as we shall see in due course, C. H. Archer and his associates have demonstrated during the last decade how wrong they all were. As we pass along the coast we shall hear from time to time what they thought of it, but before starting out on our journey it is worthwhile looking a little more closely into some of Arber's classic conclusions.

For the whole length of this coastline the watershed runs more or less parallel to it and for much of the time only a short distance inland. In consequence, nearly all the streams are short and as they have small catchment areas, carry only a small volume of water. Their power to cut down their beds cannot match the tremendous power of the sea eroding the cliffs and cutting back their mouths, so that a great number of them end in waterfalls over the cliff, the form of the fall being determined largely by the nature of the rocks. Along the hog's back coastline east of Combe Martin the finest waterfalls can only be appreciated from the fore-shore and, until the advent of Archer and Agar, had only been examined at infrequent intervals from boats. Indeed Arber, usually so meticulous over details, missed the fall in North Cleave Gut altogether. The principal falls, all 100-200 ft high, are Hollowbrook below Martinhoe, North Cleave Gut, Neck Wood Gut, Holelake below Trentishoe Down and Sherrycombe between Holdstone Down and Great Hangman. Further west, on the flat-topped cliffs just over the Cornish border Litter Water falls seventy ft clear to the foreshore, while the complex fall at Speke's Mill Mouth shows the influence of rock formation on the nature of a fall. There are a number of places along the coastline where river valleys ran at one time almost parallel to the sea's edge. As the sea cut back the cliff the valley wall was breached, causing the stream to break out through the gap and leaving the remainder of its former course isolated and dry. The best example is at Hartland Quay, where Wargery Water at one time entered the sea north of the Quay. As the sea cut back the cliff it terminated successively between Hartland Quay and Screda Point, then south of Screda Point and finally, as now, just north of St Catherine's Tor. Further north the strangely flat piece of land called Smoothlands marks the one-time course of Titchberry Water, and so on. These topographical features provide an entertaining side study for the North Devon traveller.

Page, in 1895, started his description of the coast of North Devon at County Gate, or Cosgate as he calls it, with what is now a nostalgic period piece:

Surely this broad road, wild though it be, connecting Lynton with Porlock cannot long lie desert. No—even as we gaze, a dark mass tops the distant brow, and the 'Katerfelto' coach, crowded with holiday-seekers, comes rattling towards us, drawn by four stout horses which have not yet had time to tire of the West Country hills. On it rolls, the harness jingling gaily, and the bars swinging with motion almost rhythmical with the even trot of the steeds. As it approaches Cosgate the guard executes a fanfare on the horn . . . the shining black and red vehicle swings through the gate into Devonshire, and vanishes with another fanfare round the heathery slope of Old Barrow.

Seventy years later we are likely to find this same road beset with motor cars so, not lingering as Page could over the view, we hasten to escape into the countryside. In England today the bounds of inaccessibility are dwindling as the modern motorist tackles rough lanes and tracks and even open moorland and fields in his search for adventure. The time has come to keep the motor car at bay and to safeguard what is left. The wonderful network of footpaths over our country needs to be preserved solely for foot travellers and towards this end long distance routes like the S-W P C Path can make a particularly important contribution.

The Path leaves the A39 road, then, and crosses the seaward face of Old Barrow with views across the Severn Sea to Wales and upstream to Steep Holm and Flat Holm; then on through Wingate Farm and Dogsworthy, across the north side of Kipscombe Hill and Countisbury Common to Countisbury Church. There is a loop path for those who wish to circumambulate Foreland Point and visit its lighthouse. The route now crosses the A39 again, traverses Wind Hill and traces the spine of a long ridge down to Lynmouth. The flood tragedy of 1952, when the waters of the East and West Lyn Rivers, swollen by torrential rains on Exmoor, destroyed much of the village enforced up-to-date engineering design for the rebuilding of the streamways, bridges and waterfront. It should not happen again. To reach Lynton above one can climb the wooded slopes or go up by the cliff railway, which is powered by one of the cliff waterfalls. At the top, a tank on the down car fills until the weight is sufficient for the car to descend; in the process the up car is raised, the water is discharged at the bottom and the process repeated.

The scenic highlight of Lynton is the Valley of Rocks, which runs westwards parallel to the coast immediately behind the summit ridge of the hog's back cliffs—Holiday Hill, Ragged Jack etcetera. It is the former valley of the Lyn River which once flowed on past Woody Bay to the sea further west. From Lynton the S-W P C Path takes the North Walk which traverses high up the seaward slopes of the cliffs and leads into the Valley of Rocks close to Castle Rock, beyond which there is a steep tourist path down to the beach at Wringcliff Bay. The curious rock pile known as the Devil's Cheesewring, featured in *Lorna Doone* as the home of the witch Mother Meldrum, is on the slopes opposite. The valley will be busy with cars and holiday makers in the summer months, but the road towards Lee Bay is narrow and many do not attempt it. The walker must do so, however, as there is no cliff edge path round Duty Point. We pass the secluded cove of Lee Bay and the oddly flat-topped Crock Point and so reach the tree clad slopes of Woody Bay, which fortunately escaped its one-time scheduled development as a seaside resort. In 1869 James Hannington came to the little church of Martinhoe on the plateau above, first to study and later as curate; in 1885 as Bishop Hannington he met a martyr's death in Africa. Let Page describe the part he plays in our story:

> In the intervals of study, Hannington amused himself by making a breakneck path to some caves beneath the cliff. For a while he managed to enlist the services of certain parishioners but, one by one, they left him, frightened at the dangerous character of the

work, and he and the rector's son were left to themselves. Success ultimately crowned their efforts, and Hannington 'personally conducted' many visitors to the wild shore beneath these Martinhoe cliffs.

A few years ago Archer made a determined effort to locate these paths, which are marked incidentally on the Six Inch OS Maps; he found them completely overgrown and, though the beginnings are visible in the winter when the bracken has died down, it is no longer possible to rediscover the lines with certainty. There is no doubt, however, that Hannington made routes somewhere hereabouts of which Archer himself would have been proud.

Ahead now is the deep cleft of Heddon's Mouth, the stream in which, draining a large area of Exmoor, has cut down its mouth to sea level. The flanking cliff to the east, over 800 ft high, was the site of a Roman Signal Station. The path descends from here into the valley and climbs out again on the far side either by Trentishoe Combe, or more steeply if you like, straight up from sea level by a slope worthy of any mountainside. We soon reach the seaward flank of the hog's back cliffs again and the path rolls on westwards along the slopes of the highest hills of the route— Trentishoe Down, 1,060 ft, Holdstone Down, 1,145 ft, and Great Hangman, 1,043 ft. The situation is superb and the view extensive but little can be seen of the cliff foot because the seaward slopes are convex and the vegetation prolific. Between the last two hills the path skirts Sherrycombe at a high level; indeed in summer the vegetation makes the combe impenetrable except here or very close to the cliff edge, where there is a small turfy hollow suitable for sleeping out. From here to the summit of Great Hangman is 1,000 vertical feet of precipitous hillside, of which Page writes:

So it is mountaineering now with a vengeance. I have done some of the worst of the Lake mountains. I have done Ben Nevis, but I know nothing, except perhaps the screes of Rosset Ghyll, to equal the tremendous climb up the slippery slopes of Great Hangman.

The situation of these slopes, hung between sea and sky, is as fine as that of any mountainside. Our route plunges down a ridge to the summit of the Little Hangman, a conical hill rising straight from the sea, and then along Lester Cliff into the little resort of Combe Martin, once the site of important silver mines.

From here on the cliffs are less wild and lonely. At first the main road runs near the sea's edge but we leave it at the earliest possible moment for the old road, now a footpath, and so reach Small Mouth. For the next mile or two we are never very far from the main road. At Watermouth for a change the sea has drowned the river mouth; the north-east side of the former valley is being broken down by the sea and Sexton's Burrow and Burrow Nose have already been separated off. There are caves here and fossils of the sea lily; West Hagginton, a little further on, has fossils also, as well as a variety of rocks—slates, limestones, shales and sandstones all exposed within a small area. Past Hele the route crosses Hillsborough, which gives an almost aerial view of Ilfracombe and so down into the town.

We leave again by the Torrs Walk and continue along the downs to Lee Bay, then another mile of cliff path leads past Pensport Rock to Bull Point with its lighthouse. Round Rockham Bay we come to Morte Point and the end of the north facing stretch of cliff which we have followed since entering the county. Between here and Baggy Point the famous sands of Woolacombe, which face west, provide a quite different sort of going. Baggy Point, a splendid sandstone headland with fine rock scenery at the tip, gives a delightful cliff top walk round to Croyde Bay, another popular resort. This in turn is buttressed on the south by Saunton Down, where Arber found a granite erratic boulder of seventy cubic ft believed to have come ice-borne from Scotland. Beyond Saunton Sands the S-W P C Path expires in Braunton Burrows for want of scenery and the traveller must cross the estuary of the Taw-Torridge by whatsoever route he pleases and start the walk again at Westward Ho! with its famous pebble ridge, or 'popple'.

Apart from the short section east of Clovelly traversed by the Hobby Drive, the cliffs of North Devon still ahead are all of the flat topped type. Up to Hartland Point the coastline faces north across the comparatively sheltered 'short seas of the Channel' and it is not exposed to the long fetch of the Atlantic. Beyond it, battered by 'the league-long rollers of the ocean', it is a savage coast indeed.

From Westward Ho! the first seven miles of cliff, though pleasant enough, are not specially distinguished scenically. First comes Abbotsham Cliff, which leads on to Greencliff, where outcropping coal was worked at one time. By Cockington Head is Tut's Hole, a prominent anticline in the cliffs. Past Peppercombe, where for a short stretch the rocks are Triassic reds and yellows, and Buck's Mill, we arrive at the beginning of Clovelly's famous Hobby Drive, a two mile carriage way which skirts the seaward slopes of a stretch of hog's back cliffs to finish in the upper part of Clovelly village. There are good views of the Severn Sea and over to Lundy, but almost nothing can be seen of the water's edge. Clovelly, built in a steep valley which may once have terminated in a coastal waterfall, is a place of pilgrimage for holiday makers. Exceedingly crowded during daytime in the summer months, it nevertheless retains its charm and one can of course always go at some other time. The S-W P C Path continues along the cliff top to the summit of the very steep Gallantry Bower and so down to the little cove of Mouthmill and the pinnacle of Blackchurch Rock. About four miles of steep, high cliffs now separate us from Hartland Point, which is reached by way of Exmansworthy Cliff, Chapman Rock and Shipload Bay—a quiet and lonely coastline.

Hartland Point, Ptolemy's 'Promontory of Hercules', is a turning point in the coast, the end of the Severn Sea and the beginning of the much sterner scenery of the Atlantic cliffs. The Point is around 300 ft high, according to Defoe 'a mountain-like proboscis'; the lighthouse stands on a shelf some distance below. From here to Trevose Head forty miles away stretches a huge bay in which there are no notable havens, so that in the days of sail any vessel driven inside this line in a westerly wind faced certain disaster on these shelterless shores, where the wreckers lay in wait. A former coastguard path conducts us now all the way to the Cornish border.

Just south of the Point is the rock mass known as Cow and Calf and beyond that rises the fantastic smooth face of Upright Cliff, hard by the curious flat area known as Smoothlands, of which we have already spoken. At Black Mouth a considerable stream from Hartland Abbey reaches the sea; on the far side are the high, shattered and contorted cliffs of the Warren. At one point a smooth whale-back ridge leans against the cliff face, the exposed upper face of an anticline, while nearby the twin fingers of the eighty ft Bear Rock, a foreshore pinnacle, demonstrate why we first called it Victory Pinnacle. The quay at Hartland Quay is no more, though some relics remain. Hereabouts we can see the former line of Wargery Water, which now reaches the sea just north of St Catherine's Tor, a hill formerly conical which has been slowly sliced into a half cone by the sea. Speke's Mill Mouth, with its outstanding waterfall, comes next, followed by the slabs of Brown-spear Point and the high cliffs of Mansley, Sandhole, Embury and Knaps Longpeak. Three and a half miles south of Speke's Mill Mouth is the tiny beach of Welcombe and a half a mile further over the next hill the little stream at Marsland Mouth is the county border. The length of the S-W P C Path in North Devon is about seventy miles.

CLIMBING

From the climbing point of view we can divide the North Devon coast into two areas separated by the Taw-Torridge estuary and the sand and shingle wastes of Braunton and Northam Burrows. That to the south and west is left to the next chapter where it is described alongside the contiguous cliff line which stretches on southwards from Marsland Mouth. The present section deals with that to the north and east.

The cliff foot traverse along the whole of this length, by far the longest of its kind in the country, was carried out by C. H. Archer and C. R. Agar between 1954 and 1964 and described by the former in his *Coastal Climbs in North Devon*, published privately. In 1963 they joined up with Cyril Manning and Mrs P. Harris (now Mrs Manning), who had already begun some exploration independently. Manning has been responsible for most of the harder things done since then. For Archer and Agar the beginning was casual but the ideas which gradually developed were entirely their own. It was not until later that they discovered that Arber in 1911 had advocated almost exactly what they were trying to do. Not that Arber's achievements in exploration were specially enterprising, but his attitude to the problem was most refreshingly forward-looking; it is a pity that more than forty years had to elapse before his vision of a shoreline traverse from Porlock to Boscastle came at last to fulfilment.

Archer and Agar developed this concept slowly over the exploration years. One of their great advantages was availability, for it is essential in this sort of work to be able to tackle some of the problems on days of specially low tide or during periods of specially settled weather, and this could hardly have been done by anyone who had to make set visits from a distance. During the period 1954-57 their efforts were directed towards the cliffs between Heddon's Mouth and Combe Martin; then during 1958 the coast between Woody Bay and Heddon's Mouth and between Wringcliff Bay and Lynmouth was traversed; finally between 1959 and 1961 Baggy Point and the remaining sections between Foreland Point and Morte Point were done to complete the route, which in the ensuing years was improved and simplified. Keith Lawder and I did not enter the picture until 1962, when we gave some help with the further exploration of Baggy Point; it was only then that Archer learned of the close parallel between his efforts and those of Andrews in West Penwith half a century earlier, which I shall describe in due course.

It should be emphasised that much of this terrain is not for the non-climber. It is not that the climbing problems on these traverses are particularly hard technically, but the fast movement over easy rocks, which comes from familiarity with meeting and solving the technical problems of rock climbing, is often essential in order to cover the ground in the available time. Techniques of safeguarding with the rope must be understood and mastered and, indeed, extended to deal with situations which are not normally encountered in rock climbing. The term 'climbing-way-down' the cliff is merely relative to the difficulty of the neighbouring slopes and by no means implies that it is possible to walk; in fact ropes and mountaineering-type techniques will probably be involved. Between Lynmouth and Combe Martin there are now some sixty descending lines of varying standards of difficulty, so that the competent coasteer is unlikely to be cut off by the tide anywhere along the base of these cliffs. However, the nature of the terrain does change from year to year due to rock falls, vegetation growth and so on—closing some routes, opening up others. The coasteer must be able to move safely on steep vegetation, even cut his way through it, climb and handle rock of widely variable quality, tramp over sand, stones and rounded boulders, often covered with slime and seaweed, and splash through pools and inlets. He must be prepared to use holds beneath the water, or with the water rising and falling below him, he must race the water to climb a hard place between waves, he may even have to swim. He must know all about heights and times of tides so as not to be cut off. All this amounts to experience which, methodically acquired, would in the end enable the hardest of the traverses to be accomplished safely. Great care is essential at all times as even a slight accident at the base of a 1,000 ft sea cliff might well involve most serious rescue problems.

The intending climber can survey the whole of this coast during a convenient afternoon steamer trip from Ilfracombe to Foreland Point which is run periodically throughout the summer months. Real sport for the coasteer begins just east of Foreland Point, where below and to the east of the lighthouse a path leads down to a fixed rope and so to the beach at Goat Rock. Though there is but little foreshore round the point, the rock gives excellent holds. As far as the corner, climbing is along the strata and fairly straightforward, but beyond it the climber, now crossing the strata, is forced out towards the sea. 400 yds from Goat Rock, on which there are two other climbing-ways-down on the cliff, open beach is reached. Page writes of the Gun Caverns beneath Foreland Point, three of them 100 ft long, the fourth 200 ft. Some slab climbs have been made hereabouts. Pleasant and easy going follows past Coddon Slip and Upper and Lower Blackheads to Sillery Sands, where there is a path up the cliff. An isolated rock at Lower Blackhead, fifty ft high, has not been climbed. West of Sillery is one rocky headland easily passed and then beach to Lynmouth.

In the next section access to sea level is straightforward at Wringcliff Bay, which is reached by a tourist path from the Valley of Rocks just beyond Castle Rock. The mile of foreshore traverse between here and Lynmouth is not so difficult as some of the sections further west, nevertheless Archer recommends that it should not be attempted in its entirety without preliminary exploration from the Lynmouth end. From here, after 500 yds of boulders and 700 yds of reefs, the coasteer reaches a tricky section involving wading and possibly some swimming; whichever way the traverse is being done fore knowledge of the route over this stretch is very worthwhile. The remaining 500 yds to Wringcliff is boulder-going once again. There are two other climbing-ways-down in this section, one on either side of the difficult passage. Some possibility exists of short rock climbs hereabouts on the cliff face itself; there may be something too on the Devil's Cheesewring in the Valley of Rocks.

The next cliff section from Wringcliff Bay to Lee Bay, some half a mile long, is straightforward also except for one cleft, Duty Creek, just short of Duty Point, which can only be passed dry-shod at an exceptionally low tide. On the way an easy foreshore pinnacle is passed giving good views up and down the coast. Jennifer's Cove, just beyond Duty Point, has a flying buttress at the rear which can be approached from the landward side, though the final gendarme on the ridge looks very unstable. Between Lee Bay and Woody Bay the promontory of Crock Point may require a short swim at one place, though it has been passed entirely on rock about thirty ft up. There are two climbing-ways-down *en route*, one immediately west, the other 300 yds west of the Point. A detached rock almost as high as the cliff, facing the Point at a distance of thirty yards, can also be climbed for the view; a few yards east is a cave at sea level some fifty yds long, only accessible to the coasteer.

The technical difficulty between Woody Bay and Heddon's Mouth is of a higher standard and required considerably more detailed exploration for the working out of the route. As was usual with the more difficult sections, the pioneers began at both ends probing towards the middle; later, as necessary, searching out and descending climbing-ways-down at appropriate places in between. From Woody Bay to a boulder strewn beach west of Wringapeak the climbing is straightforward; the headland itself, where there is a climbing-way-down, being passed by means of a cave. The boulder beach leads in 250 yds to a difficult section where headlands, known to climbers as Big Bluff, Double Bluff and Great Bastion, jut out from the cliff line. Between Big Bluff and Bloody Beach ahead the topography is so complex that anyone attempting a traverse must explore the difficult stretches from either side beforehand. Big Bluff, 150 ft high, is passed via a hole leading into a cave and Double Bluff by a walk on a reef at low tide or by the neck joining it to the main cliff face; the Bastion, 210 ft high, is traversed on the seaward face about twenty-five ft up. Immediately beyond Great Bastion is Hollow Brook Waterfall, which falls 120 ft sheer, followed by cascades of fifty ft and sixteen ft. A climbing-way-down close by brings the coasteer to the foreshore near the Cormorant Rock, a good viewpoint from the difficulties on either hand. After a few hundred yards of easier going another obstacle, the Pyramid, is encountered; a bluff with a hole through it and a rock bridge half way up the hole form a giant letter A. Beside this is another climbing-way-down. Hereabouts an inlet of the sea enforces a swim of ten yds, or alternatively a climb of 100 ft must be followed to the top of the Pyramid, with a descent thirty yds further on down Red Slide Buttress. From here no more wading or swimming is necessary, but the next section of 200 yds is a real climbing traverse. Finally, a long tiresome slog of 650 yds along the boulders of what was called in desperation Bloody Beach leads to Highveer Point, and an easy climb round to Heddon's Mouth. Hannington's Paths, to which reference has already been made, came down to Bloody Beach, though the exact lines have been lost. The climbing-way-down discovered at the eastern end is not necessarily one of his. Heddon's Mouth is a picturesque cove with the ruins of an ancient lime kiln and is accessible to, and popular with, holiday makers.

The headland west of Heddon's Mouth involves a scramble only and this leads to the 450 yds of boulder strewn Sker Beach, with three climbing-ways-down. Another scramble for 200 yds or so takes us on to a 500 yds stretch of foreshore named successively Ramsey Beach, East Lymcove Beach and West Lymcove Beach. Above the latter is a natural amphitheatre, about 250 yds across, which Archer has called the Horseshoe. Another climbing-way-down has been worked out hereabouts. The headland at the far end is steep, though the original swimming route has recently been circumvented on rock by an intricate traverse including two short climbs; now simple beach-going leads on to Bosley Gut, where the climbing-way-down presents no difficulties after a rubbish dump in the upper part has been left behind. We have now arrived at a much more difficult and worthy section which includes the tremendous scenery of North Cleave Gut.

All the way from Bosley Gut to Holelake Waterfall the technical difficulty is high; there are a number of places which can only be passed satisfactorily at the lowest of low tides, and as the distances between the climbing-ways-down are only just possible in the time available on any tide, accurate timing of an attack is vital. The 400 yds between Bosley Gut and North Cleave Gut give the most difficult climbing between Heddon's Mouth and Combe Martin. North Cleave Gut is an inlet over 100 yds long, a mere ten yds wide, with rock walls of 250 ft on the east and no less than 400 ft on the west. The waterfall consists of three chutes having a total height of 300 ft. Archer has written:

> Seen from below after rain, North Cleave Gut is a unique sight, even on this magnificent coast; one gets the feeling of walking up the nave of some vast natural cathedral . . . however, the approaches

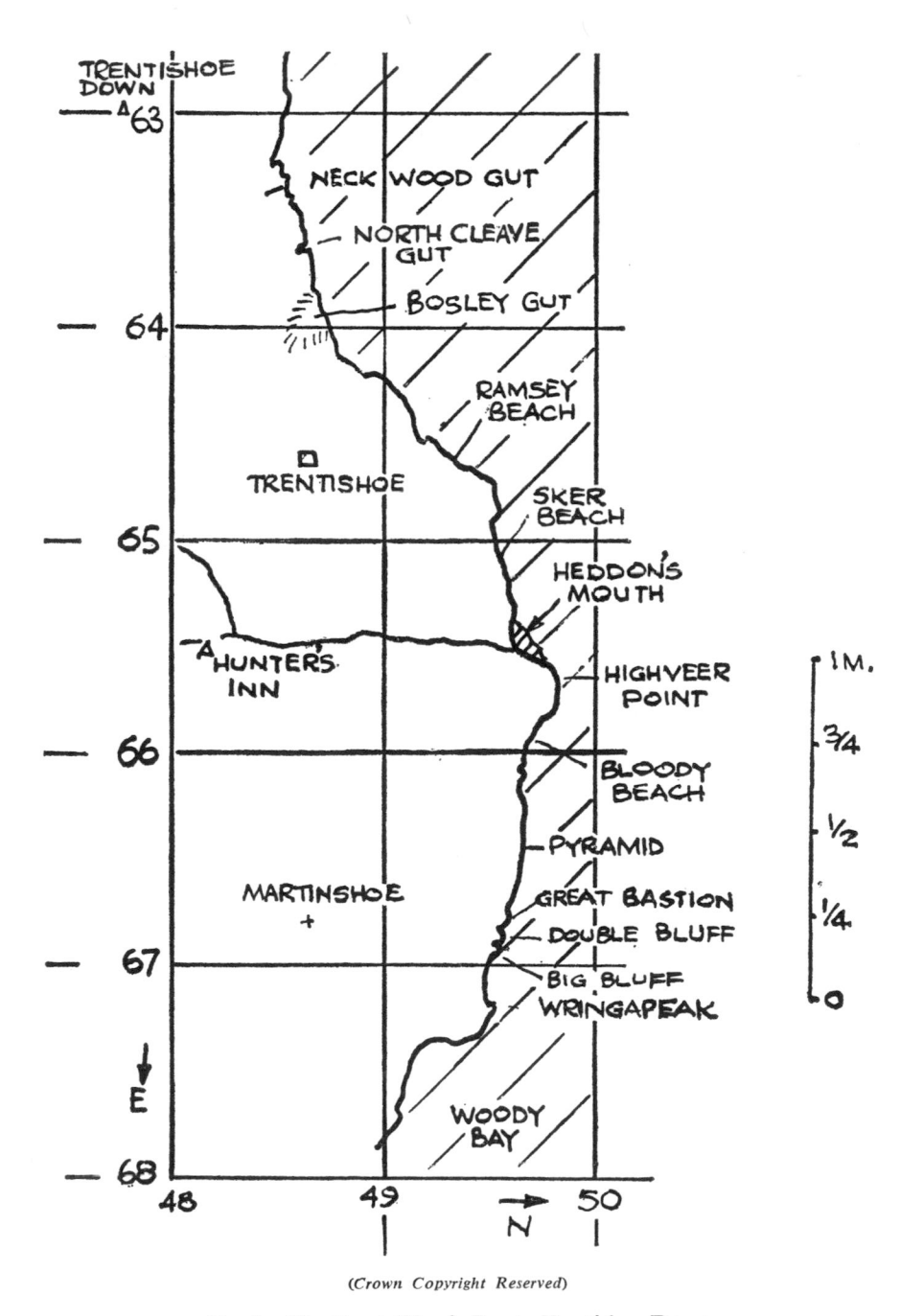

Fig 2.   The Coast, Woody Bay to Trentishoe Down

are sufficiently formidable that they should only be attempted by a strong party timing itself to take full advantage of an exceptionally low tide.

Another 1,000 yds, only slightly more amiable, intervene between North Cleave Gut and the Royal Route, a straightforward climbing-way-down just this side of Holelake Waterfall. Along this stretch the cliff has been descended in two or three places needing previous preparation with fixed ropes, while an easier one has come to light recently close to Neck Wood Waterfall. At this fall, which is in three sections of 220 ft, 17 ft and 60 ft, the early explorers used a short rope ladder below the final big chockstone. Archer had an adventure once with this:

> The ladder hung free because of the overhang, and the rungs turned out to be insecurely fixed in the wire rope on one side of the ladder. At the critical moment when I was trying to wriggle over and get a grip on top of the chockstone, they telescoped along the wire rope, forming a heap on one side—a mishap which one would suppose to be disconcerting if it happened in the middle of a precipice in the darkness of a cave! Moreover the chockstone was large and smooth and round, so that one could grip nothing except the ladder, and it lay so close along the chockstone that one's hand tended to get crushed. With the ladder swinging in wildly under the overhang, and the sliding of the rungs making it most difficult to use them at all, I had insufficient purchase to cope with the difficulties above.

He extricated himself by anchoring the foot of the ladder.

Proceeding westwards from Neck Wood Waterfall the headland beyond is passed by a tunnel or a scramble round the outside to a beach where Archer's Royal Route, very easy, comes down 100 yds short of Holelake Waterfall. This 200 ft fall lands on the debris of an old landslide and higher up are cascades. There is another climbing-way-down here that can be used without a fixed rope. Another rocky headland, traversed on the seaward side, and 300 yds of boulders lead to the Mare, ninety ft, and Colt, twin rocks—forty-five ft and sixty ft, foreshore pinnacles which give easy climbs. 300 yds more and we arrive at another climbing-way-down; a rocky headland is passed leading on to Red Cleave, a series of faults in the cliff. There is yet another climbing-way-down here and an interesting stream at the cliff top which, instead of forming a cliff waterfall, disappears into a crack in the ground, part probably of a major series of landslips, and reaches the sea by

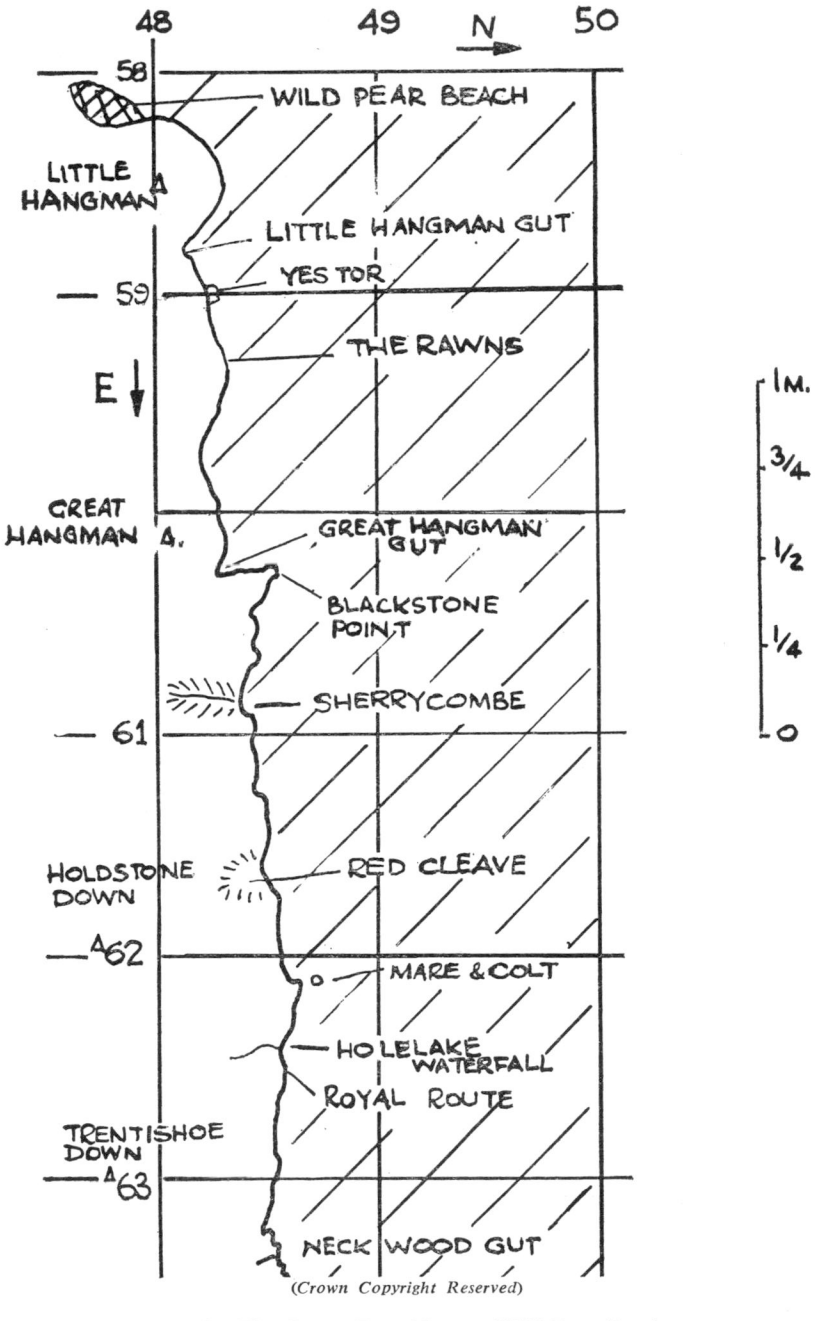

48   49   N   50

58

WILD PEAR BEACH

LITTLE
HANGMAN

LITTLE HANGMAN GUT

YES TOR

59

THE RAWNS

E

GREAT
HANGMAN

GREAT HANGMAN GUT

BLACKSTONE POINT

SHERRYCOMBE

61

HOLDSTONE DOWN

RED CLEAVE

62

MARE & COLT

HOLELAKE WATERFALL

ROYAL ROUTE

TRENTISHOE DOWN

63

NECK WOOD GUT

1M.

3/4

1/2

1/4

0

(Crown Copyright Reserved)

FIG 3. The Coast, Trentishoe to Wild Pear Beach

an underground route. Round the next easy corner is Sherrycombe Waterfall which has a larger catchment area than any of the others and in consequence carries a larger volume of water. It is 150 ft high, with a final fall of 100 ft direct to the sea at high tide; there are two climbing-ways-down to the east of it. For the next mile the going is fairly straightforward, past Blackstone Point, where there are mine adits, Great Hangman Gut, another climbing-way-down, and the Rawns, where, Page tells us, the cliff used to be descended years ago by local people collecting the seaweed known as laver. This was, and in fact still is, boiled down to a jelly and used on bread in preference to butter, or fried with bacon and eggs. The highest and most vertical cliffs on the coast, between 600 and 700 ft, are those below Great Hangman.

The final obstacle is the rocky bluff of Yes Tor (a name also given to the most prominent hill on Dartmoor) just before Little Hangman is reached. In the early years this was passed by wading and swimming, but recently Cyril Manning has discovered a route on rock involving 100 yds of unbroken traverse at two levels, the lower one only available at low tide. The material here is good, and there are some short conventional climbs of forty to sixty ft on the north face of the head; these can be approached from above by descending an easy narrow ridge from the col between Great and Little Hangman. For the next section of traverse a low tide is essential, otherwise only moderate climbing remains between here and Wild Pear Beach where there is a tourist path, and thence to Combe Martin is straightforward also.

The traverse on westwards becomes much easier, and, in fact, Archer only considered three sections to be worthy of description;

Bedruthan Steps, North Cornwall. This fine cove, seen from the cliffs to the south, has a magnificent series of foreshore pinnacles. Access to the sands is for coasteers only

these are Oakestor to Watermouth, the north-west face of Hillsborough and a 1,000 yd stretch from Torrs Point west of Ilfracombe to Hazel Bushes Bay. The climber passing through Ilfracombe should diverge for a moment to be photographed beside a council notice board which reads 'Rock Climbing is Dangerous'; indeed it can be.

Three quarters of a mile west of Combe Martin the cliff called Oakestor is 100 yds long and 200 ft high, falling straight into the sea. This has been traversed dry shod. Westwards is a series of ribs on the cliff with small detached bluffs on the foreshore below. Beyond the last of these, Hamator Rock, is Broad Strand, a sandy beach which can be approached from above by a flight of steps. There are various rock problems and some wading is needed. Further on some climbs of fifty ft have been made on the foreshore islet of Burrow Nose. On the seaward face of Hillsborough two sandy beaches—Broadstrand Beach, not to be confused with the other above, and Rapparee Cove are separated by spurs and a pinnacle. These can be passed on the outside on a very low tide, but give interesting climbing at other times. Archer describes the third section, west of Ilfracombe, as unusually spectacular. Over a distance of 1,000 yds, between Torrs Point and Hazel Bushes Bay the cliff is 300 ft high, the climbing is mostly straightforward on rock which is notably rough.

We are now approaching a historical site in coasteering, for it was here by Bull Point that Tom Longstaff, who later during a long and adventurous life climbed in many parts of the world, first practised his 'infant and nurse-escaping feet in individual enterprise':

(above) Roche Rocks, St Austell Moors. The north end facing towards the road, with the ruins of the Chapel of St Michael and a thick coating of ivy; (below) The Cheesewring, Bodmin Moor. Typical granite tor formation, first recorded ascent in the 1920s, now underpinned to prevent collapse from continual weathering

I had already been bitten by the physical urge to climb; my cousins lived on the North Devon coast facing Lundy Island. The cliffs are only slate but finely fretted by tumultuous seas. We began climbing in a small way in 1887 and by 1892 we were using a rope. Such climbs were nearly all horizontal traverses. The rules were to get round the headlands between the top of the cliffs and the sea below, keeping above high water mark if possible. There was a good climb from Thrift Cove round Bull Point to the buzzard haunted cliffs of Rockham Bay. Some of the passages were difficult. The sharp slates of 'Gory Corner', the crux of the traverse, drew blood.

This scrambling is not difficult but it is hallowed ground.

Baggy Point, between Woolacombe Sands and Croyde Bay, provides the last remaining climbing north of the Taw-Torridge estuary. Longstaff climbed here too, traversing the point at sea level before the turn of the century. In 1962 we picked a splendid route down the cliff using a long crack in a slab and felt very pleased about it. Only later did we learn that Longstaff had done it so many years before:

> The north-west corner of the traverse of Baggy Point is done by 'Scrattling Crack', a curious fault at an otherwise impassable corner. The crack is about 130 ft long, but not difficult since it is not really as vertical as it looks, and a foot or knee can always be squeezed in. It is quite exciting to race for this corner on a rising tide with a good sea running.

Archer worked out a traverse of the Point independently, discovered, explored and extended our knowledge of the complex series of caves beneath it and climbed the pinnacles—Warspite, Dragon and Coxcomb. There is a spectacular and very steep sandstone slab on the south face of Long Rock, the extreme tip of the Point. This plunges straight down into the sea and, except for the base, is as yet untrodden by climbers. Climbing-ways-down are obvious at either end of the crags, while Scrattling Crack gives a quick approach to the central area. Page writes of an early coasteer at Baggy, who was surely one of us:

> . . . another daring visitor was caught, and spent four dreadful hours climbing the cliffs, cutting notches in the shale with his pocket knife.

The whole traverse from Foreland Point to Saunton Sands is a monument to the single-minded drive of Archer and his friends. Though working independently they followed closely, to a completely successfuly conclusion, the lines predicted by Arber.

Inland in North Devon there is no recorded climbing so far; there are, however, some promising looking quarries in various places, near Bampton and Torrington for example. An ancient print, not yet identified, of 'Rocks near Torrington' shows an Alpine type arête which, if it has been accurately depicted, would be a worthy addition to the amenities.

LUNDY

Lundy is eleven miles north-north-west of Hartland Point and incidentally a mere thirty miles south of Tenby in Pembrokeshire. Three miles long and half a mile wide it runs roughly north to south and lying athwart the seaway carries a lighthouse at each end. The name is probably derived from Lund—a puffin—and Ey—an island, so that it is incorrect to speak of Lundy Island. The island tender, the *Lundy Gannet*, carrying supplies and mail, crosses from Bideford about three times a week, and weather and space permitting, passengers may travel over on this at any time of the year. During the summer months a regular service of day steamer trips (P.&A. Campbell Ltd) from Ilfracombe takes across large numbers of holiday makers who spend two or three hours on the island. Visitors booked to stay can also travel this way. There is a hotel, also a few cottages to let; the Lundy Field Society uses the Old Lighthouse as a headquarters and accommodates its members there; a strictly limited number of campers is allowed and then only by previous arrangement. Full particulars on all these points must be obtained in advance from the Resident Agent. Permission to climb must also be obtained beforehand. The island is a private estate belonging to the Harman family and visitors must remember that they are in the position of guests whatever the duration or purpose of their stay. There are no taxes on income, no rates and no licensing hours at the Marisco Arms which stays open as required. Mail posted on the island must carry, in addition to the normal postage stamp, a local stamp on the reverse side. This will be one of an attractive series of pictures of the eponymous puffin; the values are also given in puffins at a rate of one puffin equals one penny.

In the 1860s, when granite was quarried on the east coast, the population is said to have been 200. It has never reached this figure since and now numbers about 20, of which six are lighthouse keepers, while the others are concerned with the industries of the island—providing services to visitors and farming. There are about 180 acres of pasture and arable land, used mainly for potatoes and oats, the remainder is rough grazing for hill sheep. The island mammals also include red deer and Japanese Sika deer, Soay sheep and wild ponies, introduced by Mr M. C. Harman in the 1920s. There are wild goats, black and brown rats and a large number of pygmy shrews. The Atlantic Grey Seal breeds on the south coast. Most of the common sea birds nest here including razorbill, guillemot, puffin, shag, cormorant, fulmar petrel, kittiwake, Manx shearwater and various gulls. Unfortunately the gannets deserted Gannet Rock in 1900, driven away, it is said, by the foghorn on the newly built North Lighthouse. The Lundy Field Society maintains a warden in residence at the Old Lighthouse for much of the year, engaged on research into bird problems; much useful observation has been carried out. There is one indigenous plant—the *Brassica Wrightii*—a member of the cabbage family discovered in 1936.

Lundy has seen a wide pageant of history. Early man, Viking, lawless baron, pirate, smuggler and adventurer, royalist, foreign invader, Turk, Frenchman and Spaniard, have all made their mark on the island story. They have left, not only a wealth of legend, but also, more substantially, the grave of a giant eight and a half ft man, the castle of the Mariscos, Thomas Benson's Cave, and the walls built by his convicts, and many other remains to mark their various passings. At anchor in the sea, remote from both England and Wales, it slumbers quietly enough now—bird sanctuary, coasteering centre and quiet retreat from the motor car.

The landing beach is tucked away at the south end of the east coast, well protected from westerlies by the cliff walls below the South Lighthouse and Marisco Castle. There is no landing stage and passengers transfer to small boats to reach the shore. To the south of the beach are Rat and Mouse Islands, both easily accessible at low tide. The road to the top of the island slopes steeply northwards across the cliff into Millcombe where the owner's house, built in 1837, is sited in the most sheltered spot available. Turning westwards up the combe we climb out on to the plateau top at something over 300 ft. To the right is the island church, St Helen's, built by the Rev H. G. Heaven in 1897 and now somewhat weather worn. There is a staircase in the tower. A few yards further on, the square with the inn and the store behind the hotel is the centre of island life and this is the furthermost point for most of the day visitors.

A cliff top circuit of the island exploring on the way is a worthy day-long expedition and we begin it by retracing our steps to the top of Millcombe and setting out southwards. A few hundred yards ahead is Castle Hill and the ruins of Marisco Castle, believed to have been built late in the 12th century. It stands above a steep cliff, down which unwanted prisoners were returned with fatal quickness to the landing beach; there are steep cliffs on the south, too, above Lametry Bay which is not easily accessible. South of the castle is the cave where Benson the smuggler used to store his booty when he used Lundy as a base in the mid 1700s. The south coast has steep broken cliffs which, while they do not offer rock climbing, are nevertheless difficult to descend. Before reaching Shutter Point on the south-west corner there is a deep cave where the seals breed. The high, narrow entrance is difficult of access; after 100 yds it terminates in a high chamber with a shingle floor untouched by the sea. On the end of Shutter Point is the gigantic wedge-shaped Shutter Rock which has been climbed over towards the left from the earthy ridge leading out from the mainland. The rock is poor. It is also possible to swim to it. Higher up the slopes of the Point is a huge circular chasm, the Devil's Limekiln, 250 ft across, a huge funnel plunging down to sea level and so shaped, it is said, that the Shutter Rock inverted would fit exactly into it. The scenery hereabouts is superlative. The wrecking of a Spanish galleon on Shutter Rock is described by Kingsley in *Westward Ho!* Immediately round the corner rough steps lead down the cliff to the scene of a modern wreck—that of the battleship *Montagu* which went aground in a fog in 1906. The remains were visible for many years afterwards.

A hundred yds or so further on is Goat Island, a foreshore islet, rising from the beach in a small cove. The south face is a good climbing prospect, a route sloping up the north face gives fairly easy access. Another quarter of a mile of cliff, not really steep enough for the climber, leads to the Old Lighthouse on the highest point of the island, at 470 ft. Sea mists often obscured this lofty lantern and it was abandoned in the late 1890s when the present active lighthouses were built at considerably lower levels. The gallery of the tower gives a panoramic view of the island, but an ascent is no longer advisable because of the state of the staircase and the gallery handrail. A quarter of a mile further northwards a path leads down to the Old Battery which was a Trinity House fog signal station; the guns dating from William IV are still in place. Hereabouts is the western end of the so-called Quarter Wall, one of the three walls built by convicts during Benson's tenure of the island, which run from east coast to west. Beyond it is the Earthquake, a zone of walls and fissures linked traditionally, as are some other West Country sites, with the Lisbon Earthquake of 1755. We now cross Punchbowl Valley, cut by a stream flowing from a small inland pool called Pondsbury. The Devil's Chimney, a foreshore pinnacle about eighty ft high, slender and square cut, is at the back of a small cove to the right of the stream; the Needle Rock, another foreshore pinnacle of sixty ft, this time rounded and dumpy, lies at the seaward end of the cliffs on its left. Ahead, close to Halfway Wall are the Cheeses, piled-up granite tors with rounded weathered edges reminiscent of those of Dartmoor, giving a climb or two. From the climber's point of view the rock scenery improves slowly as we move north. Jutting out to sea by the Three-quarter Wall is the promontory of St James's Stone, the top easily accessible by grass slopes and easy rocks, with steep cliffs dropping straight down into the sea on the north. Beyond the next small cove is the clean smooth sweep of the Devil's Slide, 400 ft of slab rising direct from the water to the cliff top—a unique coastal feature. There are other precipitous crags beyond with a luxuriant coating of lichen much in evidence; there are foreshore islets also. The last three quarters of a mile of this western coastline gives a fine breezy cliff top walk, but the actual cliff face is sloping and of no interest to the climber. Finally we reach the North Lighthouse, below which is a cave 300 ft long.

The sloping coastline continues along the north side of the island. It is broken here and there by rock masses, the most impressive of which by far is the dramatic pinnacle called the Constable. So steep are the slopes from which it rises that this pinnacle has a short side of thirty ft, and is about double that height on the other. Gannet Rock, some quarter of a mile down the eastern side, is another foreshore islet with steep sides and a great crag on the cliff behind. Beyond is the extensive bowl of Gannet Combe, where an unusually large sedge grows in tussocks with deep channels between. The east side of the island is less impressive than the west, though visitors should look out for the Brazen Ward, one-time fortification from which the cannon were once thrown into the sea by French invaders, the Knight Templar Rock, a quite human profile on the cliff face, and the Logan Stone, which, however, no longer rocks. Presently the path runs along a shelf on the cliffs below the quarries from which the stone for the Victoria Embankment and Charing Cross Hotel, London, was obtained. In one of the quarries is a memorial stone to John P. Harman, VC, brother of the present owner, who was killed in Burma in the Second World War. Another three quarters of a mile above slopes now thickly vegetation covered sees us back in the island square once again.

Looking back it is difficult to appreciate why we did not go there much earlier to look at the climbing. Keith Lawder and I had been exploring the opposite coast of the mainland for several years, always seeing Lundy away across the sea and in fact using it for weather forecasting in accordance with the ancient rhyme:

Lundy plain, sign of rain;
Lundy high, sign of dry;
Lundy low, sign of snow.

The western outline, steep as it is, did not seem to promise anything better than we had at hand. How wrong we were! I am not sure what tipped the scales, probably when we read that the island is mostly granite. So, at length, in 1960 we became day trippers on our first visit. Among the first off the boat and ignoring the minor aspects of the scenery, over which we lingered in later years, we tore off to cover as much ground as possible. We found fine granite sea cliffs on the west coast—at first like those of West Penwith, then some even bigger, and finally others higher even than our favourite crags at Morwenstow. Our plan was to use slightly more than half the time for the journey north, thus leaving in theory ample time for return. Something went wrong and we finished the last mile at a jog-trot, spurred on by the steamer hooting for stragglers, and dashing down the steep road were just in time to join the last boat load. A new climbing ground had been discovered!

One June morning the following year the *Lundy Gannet* sailed from Bideford with what we thought was the first climbing reconnaisance party to visit the island. Later, inevitably it would seem, we found that Tom Longstaff had been already, as long ago as the nineties in fact, then again in 1903 and 1927. Our group consisted of Keith Lawder, the notable West Country climber, his brother Pat and myself—all members of the Climbers' Club, with C. E. Keys, J. Logan and R. Shaw from the Outward Bound School at Ashburton, the first at that time in charge of the School, the other two instructors there and our shock troops for the present campaign. The owner of the island, Mr A. P. Harman, was also aboard and when we reached the anchorage he set off a signal rocket as a formal welcome to our party. As well as looking closely at the possibilities everywhere we concentrated on the major isolated pinnacles which, by climbing tradition, were the first obvious objectives. The Constable, which Longstaff says he could not do, was climbed on the short side, VS, by Shaw and Logan using two pitons; the longer sides still await the climber. The same two also needed pitons to reach the top of the Devil's Chimney, VS, where the gulls usually hold council sitting in rows on the topmost block. Here a complex access problem had first to be solved on the steep cliff of mixed grass and rock behind. The Needle Rock gave a somewhat easier climb, VD, to Keith Lawder and myself, once again with complicated access down the main cliff.

Climbs were made on the north face of St James's Stone and on Goat Island, both of which gave problems similar to those of West Penwith. By Gannet Rock we scrambled down the main cliff to a point only fifty ft above the sea, but the tide prevented any attempt being made to reach the rock on this occasion. We learned subsequently that Longstaff had been there by boat; a later party found it to be accessible over the boulders exposed at low tide. There would seem to be some useful climbs. On this first visit, however, Shaw and Logan made a fine route, VS, on the main cliff here which we called Gannet's Buttress. The longest climb of the holiday was the great slab of the Devil's Slide, 400 ft, VD. We could not solve the problem of reaching the foot by traversing from a climbing-way-down, so Keith Lawder and J. Logan abseiled down from a point on the edge about halfway down. We had several times noticed how the goats (unroped) skipped across the top of the slab from right to left below the final vertical wall. When the climbers (roped) reached this they had the utmost difficulty in utilising the holds on this section, so that everyone acquired a great respect for caprine cragsmanship.

In later years several climbing parties have visited the island and fine climbing has been done below the Old Battery (seven routes of 120-200 ft), in the neighbourhood of the Devil's Slide and at two places on the east coast. Considerable possibilities remain. It is particularly interesting to look forward to a coasteering traverse of the base of the cliffs; this would take several weeks of entertaining climbing to develop and would be a worthy project. Because of their accessibility from a central base the cliffs of an island are particularly suitable for this sort of thing.

As a climbing centre Lundy has an atmosphere of its own— the rock is excellent, the feeling of pioneering is very real and the hours at the inn very accommodating.

3

EAST AND CENTRAL CORNWALL

THE HILLS

IN this chapter we shall consider the whole of the county of
Cornwall, save only the most westerly part beyond a line drawn
from Hayle to Cudden Point—the western part of the ancient
Hundred of Penwith, which, by virtue of its pre-eminence as the
chief rock climbing centre of the country is reserved, along with
the Scilly Isles, for a later chapter. This area of central and eastern
Cornwall includes about 230 miles of the county coastline, much
of the tin mining and china clay, the highest hills and some very
worthy rock climbing of recent discovery.

Of the six great granite hill masses of the West Country three
are included here—Bodmin Moor, the St Austell Moors and the
Carn Menellis Moors; the number is made up by Dartmoor to
the east and the West Penwith Moors and the Scilly Isles to the
west. The county summit is Brown Willy, 1,377 ft, on Bodmin
Moor, the highest and most extensive moorland west of the Tamar.
It is divided by the A30 trunk road which, between Launceston
and Bodmin, reaches a summit of 987 ft at Bolventor near the
famous Jamaica Inn. There are smuggling legends, though it is
hard to see what part the inn could possibly have played in an
essentially sea-going activity when sited so far inland. Luckily for
the walker, most visitors to the district confine themselves to this
road, moving along it either coming or going at the highest possible
speed. Walk away from it, then, and enjoy the amenities of the
Moor almost in solitude! The highest hills—Brown Willy, Rough
Tor, 1,311 ft, and Garrow Tor are grouped round the head of the
De Lank River, a tributary of the Camel. They are all easily
climbed and carry the typical summit rock scenery which we
associate with granite hills. On the far side is the source of the
River Fowey, beyond which the moors towards Altarnun reach

1,209 ft at Hendra Downs. That part of the Moor lying south of the A30 is divided by the River Fowey and a minor road which closely follows its valley. Dozmary Pool, where Sir Bedivere disposed of the sword of King Arthur, lies immediately west of this. The higher hills here are on the eastern side, culminating in Kilmar Tor, 1,280 ft. There are long lines of prominent summit rocks up to twenty-five ft high here, and on Trewortha and Hawk's Tors just to the north. From this fine central situation the view extends from the English Channel to the Severn Sea—Folliott-Stokes describes seeing the flashing lights of both Eddystone and Lundy during a night bivouac—and from Dartmoor and Exmoor on the one hand along the length of Cornwall to the Penwith hills on the other. Southwards stands Stowe's Hill, 1,249 ft, near the top of which is perched, says Carew, 'a heap of rocks which press one of lesser size fashioned like a cheese, and therethrough termed Wringcheese.' Later the *New British Traveller* was to identify this as 'originally a rocky deity worshipped by the ancient Druids.' Subsequently the name was overturned to become 'Cheesewring' and underpinning has been added at some time to prevent the rock doing likewise. Nearby is a large quarry, now disused, where some climbing has been done in recent years. The stones from here were taken by rail to Looe and shipped to Plymouth for the construction of the breakwater. Rather more than a mile away, to the south-east, is Caradon Hill, scarred originally by mine workings and recently even more so by a television mast. The gap between Bodmin Moor and Dartmoor is commanded by Kit Hill, over against the Tamar, once the centre of another busy mining area.

North of St Austell, the second granite mass reaches 1,027 ft at Hensbarrow Downs. This is the main china clay area of Cornwall; the clay, formed by chemical alteration of the felspar in the granite, was discovered hereabouts in 1755. The huge white heaps of waste product, hundreds of feet high, ugly and untidy from near at hand, assume from afar the picturesque appearance and proportions of snow mountains and, as a backdrop to the view, become the Cornish Alps. Some of the pits are 300 ft deep; Carclaze, one of the oldest, is a mile in circumference. There is a fine rocky tor at Roche. As Carew says:

. . . a huge, high, and steep rock seated in a plain, girded on either side with (as it were) two substitutes, and meritorious (no doubt) for the hermit who dwelt on the top thereof, were it but in regard of such an uneasy climbing to his cell and chapel, a part of whose natural walls is wrought out of the rock itself. Near the foot of Roche there lieth a rock, level with the ground above, and hollow downwards with a windy depth, which containeth water, reported by some of the neighbours to ebb and flow as the sea.

Otherwise there are few tors, though great boulders half buried in the hillside mark, perhaps, the sites of former tors. The roads run high across the hills and the summits present no problems. To the east, a famous building stone was quarried at one time at Luxulyan. Many miles to the north, across the base of the triangle of land running out to Trevose Head, the St Breock Downs of Devonian slates reach over 700 ft.

The granite moors of Carn Menellis between Falmouth and St Ives reach 825 ft. This was the chief mining area of the county and has suffered the most serious disfigurement, particularly around Redruth and Camborne. In the early years of this century the mines were still active and Baddeley and Ward could write:

> The best mine for the traveller to explore is Dolcoath. This is near Camborne Station, on a hill some 350 ft above the sea. Permission to view the workings is necessary, but the captain of the mine is most obliging in forwarding the wishes of visitors. The mine yields both copper and tin, and has attained the enormous depth of 2,250 ft.

In the end all the mines closed down, excepting only Geevor in West Penwith. Now there is a revival of interest and exploratory mining has been restarted in various places.

Lately the mines have also attracted the attention of cavers who, for want of new natural caves to explore, have turned to these old man-made workings for their sport. I hardly need to point out the potential dangers of this sort of work; yet the fact that responsible and experienced cave explorers embark on it proves at least that the risks are acceptable provided the precautions are adequate. The guiding principle must surely be that no one should go into a disused mine until he has had very considerable experience in natural caves of all types and standards of difficulty. Dolcoath is one of the many, both here and elsewhere in the county, which have been thus explored during the past decade. The cavers entered the system at a low level by the Dolcoath mine adit:

> The adit is narrow and rather low in places, making the first part of the trip uncomfortable. One consolation, however, is the fact

that the knee deep water is not cold; there are also patches of beautiful colouring on the walls.

The way continued past West Seton Engine Shaft, the William Henry Shaft of North Roskear Mine, over half a mile in, and Old Doctor's Shaft into South Roskear Mine to another adit followed to a point where the surface of the water almost reached the roof. 'At this point', says the account in the *Devon Speleological Society Newsletter*, 'the adit resembles a drain pipe. Working in such a place must have been terrible.' Sport, on the other hand, is worthy of such suffering. Leaving behind plenty of exploration possibilities for future visits, the party retraced its steps to West Seton Engine Shaft, 180 ft deep, which was climbed back to the surface using the original ladders still there in position.

The mining area extends away to the north of St Agnes, where the isolated conical St Agnes Beacon, 628 ft, commands a panoramic coastal view. Cornish legend places the giant Bolster with one foot here and the other on Carn Brea above Redruth, but is silent as to his reason for taking up this elevated stance.

THE COAST

No transition in scenery marks the Devon/Cornwall border at Marsland Mouth, and we pass on southwards over a further range of flat topped cliffs, all equally steep, wild and rocky. Almost immediately we reach a foreshore islet, Gull Rock, the first of several thus named. Because it carries a cairn it must be accessible, though certainly only at low water. In the next bay, Litter Water plunges direct to the beach with a clean drop of seventy ft, one of the most impressive of the coast waterfalls. Cornakey Cliff follows; then Yeol Mouth, with a notable climbers' cliff and a small waterfall, leads on to the gigantic Henna Cliff, over 400 ft high, the sheer face of which, unfortunately, is too loose for the climber. We have now reached Morwenstow, named for St Morwenna, whose Well was at the cliff edge close to another coastal waterfall. Higher up the valley is the well-known church of Morwenstow, far too large, it would seem, for the scattered community of farmhouses which it serves. Here, during the mid part of last century, the incumbent was the Rev R. S. Hawker, a 'character', whose name has survived even though he was never an important churchman. His writings, prolific but dull, were largely composed in his look-out which still survives on the Vicarage Cliff. Hollowed out of the earth, solidly roofed and fitted with seats and a stout door, this now looks out over one of the finest of the local climbing crags.

At the south end of the beach below is Higher Sharpnose Point, bounded on the north by the valley of the Tidna stream, which reaches the beach by a sloping trough and a vertical fall. There is a coastguard lookout on the point, no longer used, and a steep south-facing crag. Between here and Lower Sharpnose Point, a mile to the south, is Stanbury Mouth, the first really accessible sandy cove on this Cornish coastline. At one time the military used to fire out to sea from the TA Anti-aircraft School on the cliffs above. Happily this is now dispersed, though if the authorities saw fit to reinstate it no consideration of amenity or of the S-W P C Path would be likely to sway their decision. As always in preservation matters, we have to hope that no one will take back arbitrarily that which belongs to us anyway. Below the cliffs at Lower Sharpnose are great rock promontories in the shales, 80 to 100 ft high and impressive indeed when viewed from the beach. Half a mile on is Duckpool at the mouth of the Combe Valley, which runs up towards Kilkhampton. In the upper reaches at Stowe was the house and estate of the famous Sir Bevill Grenville, who won the Battle of Stamford Hill above Bude for King Charles and fell at last in the royal cause at Lansdowne.

From just south of Duckpool one can walk below half tide on sands all the way to Bude; there is a parallel cliff top path if required. There are several foreshore pinnacles along this stretch and further on, at the famous Maer Cliff, the most photographed syncline in the country, which appears in every other geology book as 'folded rocks near Bude.' This pleasant resort with fine sands is, among other things, 'Britain's Bondi' with beach life-savers who are said to include among their activities the rescue of cliff climbers. Compass Point, south of Bude Haven, and overlooking the town, has a tower and a steep sheet of slabs on the south side where there are some climbs. Efford Beacon is another great precipice, reminiscent of Henna Cliff, steep and high, but useless to the climber. There are several more slab faces and pinnacles in the next two miles to Widemouth Sands.

The cliff line, which has run from north to south ever since Hartland, now turns to the south-west and there is a cliff top path for much of the next dozen or so miles to Tintagel. Millook Haven shows violently contorted rocks in the cliff face, then, beyond Dizzard Point, there are notable coastal waterfalls—at the mouth of Scrade Water near Chipman Point and of Coxford Water between Castle and Pencannow Points. The latter, and the long promontory of Cambeak, enclose the sandy cove of Crackington Haven. The next section of cliff shows notable landslips in the lower parts, while the slopes behind rise to 731 ft at High Cliff, rated the highest cliff in the West Country. There are stacks, such as Samphire Rock, on the foreshore. At Rusey Point we leave the Upper Carboniferous rocks, the sandstones and shales of which have been with us since Westward Ho! and enter on the Lower Carboniferous rocks, mostly shales, which continue to just beyond Boscastle. Now the cliffs are hog's back type once again. South of Buckator is another Gull Rock, and at Pentargon we find the last of the long series of cliff waterfalls. The harbour of Boscastle at the mouth of the Valency River is narrow and tortuous. Some four miles of cliff path lead from here to Tintagel, which has a large hotel on the cliffs, conspicuous from twenty miles away. Several stacks are passed on the way; the one called Long Island, which is specially impressive, is cut off by the sea at all states of the tide, but the cairn on the top shows that it has been climbed somehow. Rocky Valley, at Bossiney Haven, is well worth exploration. Tintagel, with the fragmentary ruins of a castle on an unusually striking site, is a place of pilgrimage for holiday makers; by way of contrast the coast on southwards is little visited. We come to Trebarwith Strand, and yet another Gull Rock, 133 ft high, and then six miles of coast at present more or less trackless lead to Port Isaac. Past Porth Quin is the National Trust's Pentire Point, where the scenery, in various igneous type rocks, is impressive. This is the eastern shore of the estuary of the Camel and there are magnificent sheltered sands around Polzeath. The traveller by the S-W P C Path crosses by ferry to Padstow and resumes his walk out to Stepper Point—the western tip.

The next stretch of coastline is very fine indeed; the cliff top is straightforward enough, but a traverse at sea level has never, as far as I know, been attempted. Pepper Hole is a 200 ft funnel from cliff top to sea level, nearby is Butter Hole and a little further on at Gunver Head, Seal Hole. We are close now to Tregudda Gorge, the striking cleft between Lower Merope Island and the main cliff; further out Middle and Higher Merope Islands present access problems which have not so far been tackled. All three are over 150 ft high. A short way ahead, Porthmissen Bridge is pierced by two arches, while the Marble Cliffs next to the west are horizontally banded and have sea caves below. A number of delightful sandy beaches lie between here and Trevose Head which, with its lighthouse, marks yet another change of direction in the coastline.

The next ten miles, running more or less north and south, form a popular holiday coast which terminates abruptly at the estuary of the Gannel immediately beyond Newquay. Hockin, in fact, in his coastline walk advocates missing this part out altogether by passing inland from Wadebridge along St Breock Downs and regaining the sea beyond the Gannel. Halfway down from Trevose the cove known as Bedruthan Steps, between Diggory's Island to the north and Pendarves Island to the south, has several foreshore pinnacles and islands including the famous Queen Bess Rock. The name of the cove is of doubtful origin, but more recently was applied to a rock staircase which leads down to the beach; this has been closed for the last few years since a boy was killed there by a rock fall. Downward access nowadays is by a tricky and exposed scramble a little further north and is for coasteers only; the quality of the cliff must always be suspect, though the beach pinnacles are sound and probably climbable. At Trevalgue Head, between Watergate Bay and Newquay, there is a blowing hole which sprays water from a cleft in the cliff, and huge caves called the Banqueting Hall, the Cathedral and the Boulder Cavern. Newquay has all the advantages and disadvantages of a really great resort—wonderful

---

Wicca Pillar, West Penwith. Keith Lawder, appropriately clad for coasteering in shorts, knee pads and plimsolls, on the Edge Climb (VD)

sands and traffic jams, surfing and life savers, plenty of accommodation and large numbers of visitors.

We cross the Gannel by stepping stones at low water, or by ferry, and continue to Kelsey Head. The scalloped pattern of the coastline continues—a north/south stretch gradually swinging round to east/west, then a prominent headland and an abrupt change back to north/south. The next of these sections runs from Kelsey Head round to St Agnes Head, another eight miles of coastline. Soon we come to Holywell Bay, where in addition to the well there are two fine foreshore pinnacles, unclimbed so far. The nearer one is called, from its cowl-like overhangs, the Monk; the other further west has no name, yet deserves one. Offshore is the inevitable Gull Island, which seems to follow us on our way. Further on, Perran Beach is backed by extensive sand dunes. We are now approaching the mining area—derelict chimneys and engine houses, spoil heaps and the occasional open shaft to look out for and avoid. The pleasant resort of Perranporth is here and close by, on Cligga Head, is the first granite sea cliff; unfortunately the top has been devastated by Nobel's Explosive Works, formerly sited there, and by mining, not only ancient but modern also, for this is one of the places where they are taking another look. St Agnes Head below the Beacon looks out across the sea to the islands of Man and His Man, a mile offshore.

Another scallop of ten miles takes us to Godrevy Point and St Ives Bay. On the way the Tobban Horse at Porthtowan is an interesting looking foreshore islet; at Nancecuke nearby the course of the S-W P C Path is uncertain, for access to the cliff edge is barred at the present time. The small port of Portreath has another

---

Chair Ladder, Tol Pedn Penwith. A climbing party having crossed one of the characteristic zawns sets out on the Pegasus climb (HS)

F

Gull Rock; then follows a magnificent range of flat-topped cliffs over Carvannel Down, Reskajaege Down and Hudde Down to Hell's Mouth. It seems likely that the foreshore can be traversed for all of this distance and these fine cliffs would make such an expedition very worthwhile. There are a number of foreshore islets, too, Crane Islands, 91 and 148 ft, Samphire Islands, 126 and 121 ft, etcetera. The road at Hell's Mouth comes close to the cliff edge and there is an easily accessible view of the tremendous drop into the steep-sided cove below, with no obvious easy way down close at hand. Off Godrevy Point is an island with a lighthouse, and this side of St Ives Bay carries extensive sand dunes.

Leaving the continuation of the S-W P C Path into West Penwith for our next chapter we cross the narrow isthmus to Marazion and pick it up again close to the beginning of its course along the south coast of the county.

The path starts at Albert Pier at Penzance and runs round the sands of Mount's Bay to Marazion, a paradise for the pebble collector, who may, it is said, chance on samples of various semi-precious stones. St Michael's Mount, though smaller than its counterpart in Normandy, is much more attractive. A foreshore island connected to the mainland by a causeway, it was Ictis, the port from which Cornish tin was shipped in ancient times; later a priory and a castle were built on top. Now there is a small village and harbour below the castle, the whole of it in the care of the National Trust. The island could be circled at sea level without great difficulty—there may be climbs but they are not accessible. For the next few miles there follows a succession of sandy beaches—Perran Sands, Prah Sands, with Pengersick Castle ruins, Porthleven Sands and the celebrated Loe Bar where a pebble bank across a river mouth has produced an extensive lake immediately behind the beach. In between these the granite has its last fling at Rinsey and Trewavas Heads, while Prussia Cove and Bessy's Cove close to Cudden Point were both famous smuggling sites.

We are now starting on a circuit of the Lizard peninsula, the most southerly part of the mainland of England. For south Cornish people the peninsula is a weathercock—'when Lizard is clear, rain is near'. This certainly seems true in the view from Penzance. When it is clear, a very flat tableland of average height 250 ft is revealed, with a summit only 100 ft higher at Goonhilly Down, a vital link in the latterday urge for an international exchange of television programmes. North of a line from Polurrian Cove to St Keverne the rocks are Devonian, to the south of it mainly serpentine and hornblende schist. The cliffs are flat-topped types and there is an old coastguard path for most of the way round.

We pass on from Loe Bar to Gunwalloe and soon the cliffs begin in earnest. Poldhu, ahead, was the eastern end of Marconi's first transatlantic radio transmission; the relics are gone, but a monument remains. There is striking scenery at Mullion with Mullion Island offshore and Gull Rock, a foreshore pinnacle, below Mullion Cliff. Hereabouts is the only serpentine in a cliff line which is predominantly schist all the way from Polurrian Cove to beyond the 200 ft Predannack Head. Serpentine then reappears as far as Kynance Cove and we pass on the way Gue Graze where steatite (soapstone) was quarried, the cliff foot cave of Pigeon Ogo and a precipitous promontory called the Horse, described by Ffolliot-Stokes as 'a jagged edge of rock fangs that defies the rock climber.' Kynance, says Burton, 'is Cornwall's most famous cove . . . Asparagus Island, Mulvan, Tailor, Man o' War, Steeple Rock, the Parlour, the Devil's Letter Box, the Devil's Bellows, the Drawing Room, the Devil's Mouth—are but a few of the distinguishing features'. All these—pinnacles, caves, blow holes and so on—add up to a fascinating scenery, but it is very popular with visitors and climbing would only be possible out of hours or out of season.

The cliffs on the south of the Cove again reach 200 ft; close by is Lion Rock, the accessibility of which is unknown. Schistose cliffs continue round England's most southerly headland with little in the way of climbing prospects, except on the west-facing side near the Quadrant. There is a lifeboat station and a lighthouse, while inland at Lizard Town the local serpentine is worked into a wide range of take-home objects for tourists. Between here and Cadgwith there are several sea caves—Chough's, Ravens' and Dolor Hugo's, as well as two huge funnel shaped depressions going down from the cliff top to sea level, the Lion's Den at Housel Bay and the Devil's Frying Pan at Cadgwith. The latter is some 200 ft deep, and it is possible to enter the lower reaches at sea level and to land on the beach at the base of the hole. The high cliffs continue to Black Head which, at 230 ft, is the boldest headland between the Lizard and Falmouth. Just beyond Manacle Point the S-W P C Path makes one of its few diversions inland to avoid

quarries on the cliff face. After passing Gillan Harbour we round
Dennis Head to a ferry on the Helford River.

Between Lizard and Coverack the cliffs are mostly serpentine with
a little granite at Cadgwith and Kennack and some gabbro at
Carrick Luz. Lower cliffs continue to Porthoustock, then a little
more schist, until we finally reach the Devonian rocks—pastures
and rolling hills around the Helford River replacing the moorland
of Lizard.

The traveller on the Path is now faced with a wide estuary,
formal and more orderly scenery, people, houses and gardens. He
crosses to Mawnan by ferry and over Rosemullion Head to
Falmouth Bay and, skirting this, arrives on Pendennis Point, the
southern arm of Falmouth Harbour. About 1540, Henry VIII
began a systematic fortification of the south coast of England; the
defence works which he caused to be built, though subsequently
called castles, were in fact artillery forts with low walls and loop-
holes for cannon. Two of the finest face one another across
Carrick Roads, one here on Pendennis Head and the other, which
has been described as an architectural gem of the Tudor period, on
the opposite side at St Mawes. In the Civil War both were held
for the King but saw little fighting; both played brief defensive
roles in the great Wars of this century. A ferry takes us across
the Estuary to St Mawes on the peninsula of Roseland; a further
ferry over the Porthcuil River and we are on Zone Point ready to
resume the coastwise tramp.

Though the S-W P C Path will eventually, we hope, provide a
right of way all along the cliff top here, there are some difficulties
in places at the time of writing. In general, this southern coast
is less wild than that of the north and cultivation tends to
occupy the terrain where the cliff top walker seeks his routes.
Gerrans Bay lies between Zone Point and Nare Head; the latter
shows some of the most promising rock exposures, actually of
igneous types, along the south Cornish coast. The offshore stacks
of Gull Rock, Middle and Outer Stones are igneous also. Veryan
Bay between here and Dodman Point has outcrops of the same
rocks and there are sandy coves, among which Kiberick and Porth-
luney are outstanding. The Dodman is a real promontory, three
quarters of a mile long and 373 ft high, very steep on the west
side. There are remains of ancient fortifications and an extensive
view.

Though a pleasant coast indeed the remainder of the Path from here to Plymouth is less likely to provide those wild, rugged features which are most attractive to the coasteer. There are four outstanding ports for the visitor—the fishing village of Mevagissey, the historic anchorage of Fowey, where there is yet another of King Henry VIII's castles, the widely famous Polperro and the facing twin towns of East and West Looe. There are industrial ports too, at St Austell and Par close to the Cornish Alps. There is a wide variety of rock types—the bright coloured green and red slates at Talland Bay being of special interest. There are cliff walks and sandy beaches with foreshore and offshore islets which may well prove attractive to the coasteer at some time; for the present, however, his attention is likely to be fully occupied elsewhere. And so finally to Rame Head, with its chapel, St Michael again, and earthworks, the western arm of Plymouth Sound. The total distance from Penzance is about 130 miles.

Standing on the Hoe at Plymouth we look out over Britain's naval history with everything from Drake to the most up-to-date present around us. Here stands the third of the Eddystone Lighthouses, the one built by Smeaton, which had to be removed when the reef began to crumble, and was re-erected here. From its windows the Douglas Lighthouse, which now guides the mariner to this historic haven, is a pillar on the horizon. The story of the earlier works by Winstanley and Rudyard is an epic which must be read for itself.

THE CLIMBING

In the twenty miles between Clovelly in North Devon and Widemouth Bay in Cornwall are the highest and most impressive cliffs in the West Country. Though this is now a major climbing area, its history is, nevertheless a short one. Haskett Smith, first to notice the climbing potential of so many places, wrote in 1894 '. . . much of the coast from Clovelly right away to Bude in Cornwall is remarkably fine', but it was half a century later before anyone tackled actual climbing problems here. Then at last in 1945, E. M. Hazelton, in the *Fell and Rock Climbing Club Journal*, described some routes he had made during the previous two years on the cliffs of Compass Point at Bude and the beach pinnacles of Sandy Mouth and Northcott Mouth. But this was an isolated effort,

Hazelton himself never returned and nothing further was done until Keith Lawder and the writer came on the scene in 1956. On our way to West Penwith that year we decided to take a longer route and look at the famous cliffs of Morwenstow, which from descriptions in non-climbing accounts sounded attractively promising. We walked from Hawker's church through the fields to the edge of Vicarage Cliff—it falls away abruptly in a near vertical wall into the cove of Lucky Hole which is bounded on its north side by a rocky promontory. There, ahead of us on the flank of the upper part of the promontory, was a sheet of rock slabs with a jagged crack running up close to the edge. Would it go? On that occasion we came and we saw, but we had other things to look at elsewhere and a programme ahead in West Penwith, so that it was not until the following year that we returned to conquer. We scrambled from the cliff top along and down the landward edge to the foot of the slab, which is separated from the beach below by a vertical crumbling wall, then made our climb up the prominent crack close to the seaward edge. We called this Hawker Slab, because it is immediately in front of his lookout which would make an excellent grandstand; it gives about 200 ft of climbing of VD standard.

Our subsequent explorations along this coast, at least on the south side of Hartland Point, revealed a pattern in the crags which enabled us to divide them into groups as follows:

> Type A. South facing sheets of slabs or walls on a promontory. The north side is often broken and at easier angle. Sometimes the same formation is found facing the other way.
> Type B. Overlapping slabs (akin to Botterill's Slab on Scafell or to Clogwyn du'r Arddu West Buttress) facing south on a cliff face. These are always found at the landward end of Type A promontories and frequently alone also.
> Type C. Beach Pinnacles, upright survivors of more resistant strata.
> Type D. Clean-cut chimneys formed by the erosion of a soft stratum from between two harder.

Very good climbs sometimes finish with a short wall of loose earth and boulders at the cliff top and this should, if possible, be examined and broken down from the top before beginning the climb. We once turned back eight feet from the cliff top when faced with this sort of problem, an occasion when we were carrying neither slater's pick nor ice axe.

Apart from an ascent of Blackchurch Rock at Mouthmill, which gives an eighty ft climb of M standard on its easy side, no climbing has been done so far between Clovelly and Hartland Point. The steep seaward face of Blackchurch and the huge precipice of Gallantry Bower, the Clogwyn du'r Arddu of the West Country, are too hard for our generations, though possibly within the powers of a younger. Beyond Mouthmill no climbing exploration of the cliffs has yet been made and there may well be possibilities. At Hartland Point the crags near the lighthouse are impossibly crumbly, while on southwards a pinnacle which protrudes in advance of the cliff line—is it the Cow or the Calf?—can be reached by a climb which is hardly even moderate. A mile or so of cliff, largely unexplored so far, which may have some prospects, leads on to Hartland Quay where there are several items of interest.

In the second cove north of the Quay is a unique pinnacle, which we originally called Victory Pinnacle; later, we found that the local name is Bear Rock. This consists of two almost parallel vertical strata formed into a chimney by the disappearance of a softer stratum between, types C and D. Standing isolated on the foreshore, it is about seventy ft high and was climbed in 1962 by R. Lewis and D. Findlayson. Their route is on the south face of the lower flake, stepping across at the top to the summit of the higher one; we looked at this later but thought the rock looked too loose for us. There is every possibility that the chimney between the flakes could be climbed by thirty or forty ft of knee and foot wedging by anyone used to this sort of work, say from practice at High Rocks, Tunbridge Wells. Between Bear Rock and the main cliffs is Consolation Pinnacle, which is lower and has a much easier chimney. On the north side of this cove Disappointment Slabs, type B, have almost provided a climb—we retreated from a point only eight feet from the top, unable to surmount a near vertical earth and stone bank. A little preparation at the top would soon convert this to an orthodox climb; the slab pitches below are quite delightful. The left edge of this slab is bounded by a rock rib which is peculiarly rounded on its north side. Though startling to look at it does not seem to provide anything useful to the climber. There are other small unclimbed pinnacles around.

At Screda Point, immediately south of Hartland Quay, are two prominent pinnacles—clean and sound on the north, broken and vegetation covered on the south. Both are isolated only at high tide. The routes here were made by Tom Patey and party in

1959. Screda Inner Pinnacle gives a route of fifty ft at its north-east corner, mild S. Screda Outer Pinnacle has a slender rock, the Needle, on its north face. The Needle gives an eighty ft climb, VS, up the right hand edge. The chimney between the Needle and the main pinnacle, the Needle's Eye, could probably be climbed. Nearer to the Quay is a knife-edged blade of rock—the Cleaver—which gives some eighty ft of climbing along the edge, MD. At Speke's Mill Mouth, the cove of the waterfall is bounded on the south by Brownspear Point. On its south face is a large expanse of slabs, type A, where three routes were made by R. Lewis and D. Findlayson centring round a cave-like indentation in the face. We later repeated one of these and considered it somewhat harder than the standard of VD assigned by the pioneers.

Between here and the Morwenstow district there are no definite routes yet, but in places some real prospects await, for instance in the neighbourhood of Knaps Longpeak. South of Marsland Mouth, the promontory behind Gull Rock is a type A crag unexplored so far. There is a cairn on the Rock itself and we have heard of an ascent, but it seems only accessible at very low water.

Half a mile further on there is a really fine type B crag at Yeol Mouth below Cornakey Cliff. At the end remote from the sea is the long narrow Wreckers' Slab, more than 300 ft long and VS. When climbed by Tom Patey, J. H. Deacon and Keith Lawder in 1959 this was the longest sea cliff route in the West Country, but it was later deposed by the Devil's Slide on Lundy. There are three long pitches and pitons were used for belays. The third slab from the sea, Smugglers' Slab, gave a 200 ft route to the same party, with two very long pitches and a standard even higher than the first climb, while further left a 160 ft climb of VD standard was later added to the tally.

As already described our first climb in the area was made on Hawker Slab at Morwenstow, a type B slab, in fact, at the landward end of a type A promontory. Halfway along the promontory on the south side a tower leans against the face. Vicarage Tower Climb follows the wall beside the Tower, traverses sensationally along the top of the promontory and then goes up a rib edge to the cliff top. This rib is actually the upper edge of a series of very thin rock strata and the nature of the rock beneath the climber's hand changes every few feet, an entertaining progress.

Between here and Hawker Slab another scrappy slab climb comes up from the beach.

At the other end of the cove, beyond the Tidna, is the out-jutting headland of Higher Sharpnose. This has some fine crags facing west and south-west on the seaward side. There are two climbs so far and prospects of more. The Quarter Deck gives nearly 300 ft of VD climbing on the largest of these slab faces. There are three pitches, but the angle eases after the first eighty ft. The second route, Bubbly, is further to the left and shorter.

A rather dull coastline follows as far as Stanbury Mouth, where one or two short routes have been made from the beach. Lower Sharpnose Point, which bounds this to the south, has some very fine rock scenery, which can only be appreciated from below. We looked from the top and decided that there was nothing much there, but J. C. H. Davis and J. J. Whitehead, probing along the beach in 1963, discovered the very fine possibilities. There are several steep-sided walls of rock with flat tops and near vertical ends running out horizontally from the cliff face; six climbs were made, other good prospects remain.

The next climbing is one and three quarter miles further south at Sandy Mouth, where a number of interesting pinnacles rise from the sands. Close to the mouth of the stream is the Flame, 100 ft high, with one route so far, while on its seaward side rises the sixty ft Square Block, which has been ascended by three different ways. All the pioneering here was done by E. M. Hazelton in 1943-44. A few hundred yards further north is Ship Ashore, a thirty-five-forty ft pinnacle which gives a climb on the landward arête. On the cliff behind is a magnificent unclimbed type D chimney, rather wide and in need of gardening at the exits to its pitches. Further north still are several smaller pinnacles, some unclimbed, and one higher, close under the cliff, which is very rotten; it was climbed to a point as near to the top as was felt to be safe. Beyond this is a type B slab which has been climbed to half height.

Three quarters of a mile nearer Bude is Northcott Mouth, where the routes are once again due to E. M. Hazelton. Towards the south end of the beach is a pinnacle of some thirty to forty ft, the Unshore, or Smooth Rock with two routes. The beach is bounded at this end by a rock wall which faces (unusually) north; this has a fifty ft chimney towards the seaward end, which has been climbed; the rest looks impossible. Round the corner is Maer Cliff, unclimbed, followed by a broken area known as the Landslip. Soon we come to two more pinnacles. The more northerly, the Horn of Plenty, is a perfect example of the profusion of holds produced in some sandstones by weathering. The seaward arête gives a VD climb which, though steep, has holds all over it. The other pinnacle, Easy Street, is only M by the sea arête. There is a promising looking slab on the main cliff here and another at Wrangle Point near Crooklets Beach, both need a preliminary clean at the top. Lion Rock at Crooklets Beach gives some fifty ft climbs.

Compass Point, the south headland of Bude Haven, is a fine type A promontory. E. M. Hazelton, who made three routes here, describes the crag as consisting of 'vertical sheets, like four mammoth playing cards standing on edge, each six or eight ft thick.' The Arête follows the seaward edge, the Face Climb is just round the corner, while the South Climb is on the most southerly of the sheets. There seem to be other prospects. In 1962 the cliff was climbed at a point about 300 yds south of the Point by B. Tondeur, Keith Lawder and the writer; this is Local Enterprise, VD, and gives a good example of how fine lines can be worked out in the middle of loose and unsuitable looking areas of cliff by any-one who has an eye for this sort of thing. So far nothing has been done further to the south. There are several type C pinnacles. Two of close to 100 ft, near Higher Longbeak, seem a little too rotten to be of interest; it is, in fact, a puzzle how they have survived at all. There are others lesser and possibly more worthy. There are numerous type B slabs, not yet by any means exhaustively explored.

Investigation has really only just begun in this very worthy coasteering area between Clovelly and Widemouth. The southerly part should have a special appeal for the family climber, for every-where south of Stanbury the crags rise straight from the sands of bathing beaches. The quality of the rock shows wide variations and the number of routes is always going to be small with large areas which are completely unusable. It is useless to judge this as if it were mountain rock and in general routes which look easy to a mountain trained climber turn out to be fairly difficult, while those which look difficult often prove impossible. Except low down close to the sea there is loose rock even on the crags which are relatively sound; this needs climbing traffic to clear it away, very much as our mountain rocks were cleaned up in the early days of rock climbing. The weather is good here and the surroundings are marvellous.

Along the whole length of the remainder of North Cornwall, from Widemouth to St Ives Bay, only one climbing route has been recorded so far. This is a chimney climb of about eighty ft on a small crag on Com Head, one mile east of Pentire Point. There is no lack of possibilities; it just happens that detailed explorations of crags which have access problems, involving perhaps approaches by boat, take a long time to work out and only an increase in the numbers of coasteering enthusiasts will produce any considerable change in the situation. Though some of the foreshore pinnacles have certainly been climbed—they have summit cairns for example —there are no definite records of ascents of such isolated peaks as the Long and Short Islands at Boscastle, the three Merope Islands at Gunver Head, Padstow, the several beach pinnacles at Bedruthan, the two at Holywell Bay, all the various Gull Rocks and many others. Apart from these, the most promising places to look would appear to be around Boscastle, on Pentire Point, around Cligga Head and St Agnes Head and near Hell's Mouth, but it is hard to be really specific without very close personal inspection. Foreshore traverses of course would give possible sport, independent of the quality of the main cliffs, at any place where the sea comes high enough to ensure that there is no backshore and where there are a sporting number of obstacles on the foreshore.

On the south coast we start with two minor granite headlands, Trewavas and Rinsey Heads, where there may be some short climbs. The Lizard is more promising—the hornblende schist cliffs in particular, notably at Predannack Head, the Quadrant (Lizard Point) and near Landewednack look likely to produce some climbs. We did, in fact, make a somewhat characterless route of about 200 ft at Predannack some years ago. The other major outcropping rock is serpentine, the basis of the local industry in polished stone ornaments, which has a tendency to be very easy angle or very steep. It occurs in possibly climbable form at the Horse, near Kynance, elsewhere round Kynance Cove, on a promontory east of Cadgwith and again north at Coverack. There are several pinnacles and islets, notably at Kynance and Mullion, also large numbers of summer visitors. At Carrick Luz near Kennack there is even thirty ft of gabbro, an almost sacred climbing rock which forms the famous Cuillin Hills of Skye. Some climbs have been done at Black Head. The coast between Falmouth and Plymouth has only a little for the climber so far. There are slight possibilities on pillow lava at Nare Head, near Portloe, while the Gull Rock offshore, when reached by boat, offers scrambling on arêtes and pinnacles and a cavern. There may be something on the Dodman. Climbing was done during the 1920s by local mountaineers, D. G. Romanis and C. B. Jerram, at various points along the Polperro coast—notably Chapel Cliffs, Noland Point and Blackybale Point to the west and Smugglers' Cove and Landslip Cove to the east. Of these, Landslip Cove would appear to be the best prospect. Again foreshore traverses might provide sport for the diligent searcher all along this coastline.

At Roche, one and a quarter miles north-north-west of Hensbarrow summit, is a massive tor surmounted by the ruins of a chapel dedicated, as are most holy buildings on hill tops, to St Michael. Legend has it that this was the refuge of the giant Tregagle 'when hunted by the Black Huntsman and his fiery-eyed pack'. Perhaps this was an allegory predicting the future invention of the motor car and its influence on lovers of the countryside. Roche is one that the great Haskett Smith failed to find and it was first described by D. G. Romanis and C. B. Jerram in the *Climbers' Club Journal* in 1923. The main mass, roughly rectangular in plan, is sixty ft high in places. None of the surrounding rocks reaches above fifteen feet. An iron ladder enables the active tourist to look over the chapel and enjoy the view over the moors and the china clay heaps, while it enables the prospective climber on the rock itself to arrange a top rope if required. About a dozen lines of ascent have been worked out, but we omit details so that readers can still enjoy the delights of pioneering. There are no nail scratches yet and need never be. In spite of the ready access this is private property and removal of vegetation from the rocks is forbidden.

There is rock scenery of great interest to the climber in the valley of Luxulyan, a few miles inland from Par. Half a mile below Luxulyan village the valley is spanned by the venerable Treffry Viaduct, 657 ft long and 90 ft high, which stands on beautiful slender stone pillars, an engineering wonder of the Railway Age. Formerly it carried the produce of a quarry on the eastern hillside away to the cross-country railways or to the sea at Par; now it is a footpath and a leat. The quarry, overgrown now with vegetation, has yielded a few climbs, while away to the south, through the woods near Carmears Waterfall, is another small crag where some forty ft climbs have been made. The real interest hereabouts is in the giant blocks—'not boulders', says Baddeley, 'but blocks'. Haskett Smith quotes the statistics and then adds comment in his own inimitable style:

> According to Mr Baddeley, here is the largest block in Europe, larger than any of the famous boulders at the head of the Italian lakes, and it may take rank with the largest known, the Agassiz blocks in the Tijuca mountains near Rio de Janeiro. He gives the dimensions as forty-nine ft by twenty-seven ft with seventy-two ft girth, yet makes no allusion to the Bowder Stone in Borrowdale, which in another work he describes as being sixty ft long, thirty ft high and weighing 1,900 tons. It would appear, therefore, that the Bowder Stone is considerably larger than the largest stone in Europe without being so remarkable for size as another stone in England.

The rock is a special form of granite known at luxulyanite, and the Wellington sarcophagus in St Paul's crypt was made from it. In locating these monsters the problem for the modern climber lies in the density of the local vegetation. Baddeley's direction for the largest is 'behind the old smithy, twelve minutes from the Viaduct, five minutes from the quarry,' but it is delightfully quiet country even if you do not find anything. Three miles away to the north Helman Tor gives some scrambles on granite.

The remaining rock outcrops are all on or around Bodmin Moor. Some two miles south of Camelford two granite buttresses, the Devil's Jump, face one another across a small valley. The eastern one gives only scrambling, but the western has a seventy ft climb up each of its front corners with an overhanging face in between. The tors on the hill tops on the main part of the Moor would give odd scrambles to the passing walker, but there is nothing of any length to tempt the climber to come specially. While hereabouts we should perhaps take note of the Old Delabole Slate Quarry—a vast hole in the ground some 500 ft deep, a striking and quite unusually ugly piece of man-made scenery. There may be climbing here one day depending on the quality of the strata left behind by the quarrymen; similar features in North Wales are already being used by climbers. The eastern Moor is more attractive rockwise. The summit tors of Kilmar, Hawk's, Trewortha and Bearah Tors were explored by R. G. Folkard during 1941. The best climbing is on Hawk's Tor, where there are at least a dozen routes of twenty ft or so, mostly of easier standards. The Cheese-wring was climbed in the 1920s by D. G. Romanis and C. B. Jerram, but there seems little point in repeating it now that the quarry beneath has at last been deserted by the quarrymen. Climbers from Truro School have made about fifteen routes there since 1964, mostly 60 to 100 ft with a few a little longer on the fine granite faces that have been left behind. It is a worthy addition to the local amenities. Permission to climb has to be obtained beforehand from the Duchy of Cornwall Office at Liskeard.

4

WEST PENWITH

TRAVELLING by the A30 trunk road through the dull and ever narrowing hinterland of Cornwall past the mining scars of Redruth and Camborne, we come at last to the wide spaces of Connor Down. The road descends a long gentle hill towards the sands of the Hayle Estuary, the foreground view marred by a sprawl of industrial development. However, it is what lies beyond that takes all the attention and quickens the pulse—a solid block of high moorland, which appears to close the whole peninsula, the gateway to the finest coastline in the county:

> A neck of land that stretches towards the west,
> Where Zennor Hill stands up to take the breeze
> That sets its myriad bracken fronds a-quiver,
> From the twin gateways of the Channel Seas.
> Its granite has the strength that granite gives,
> A Moorland and a harsh land that breeds men,
> Who seek their fortunes at the world's far end,
> And never rest till they come home again.

The low-lying land ahead running from Hayle to Marazion here demarcates the peninsula known as West Penwith, on all other sides the sea is its boundary. This is the wildest part of Cornwall—magnificent castellated sea cliffs, miles of fine moorlands, sands, the relics of ancient man and of old abandoned mine workings and, finally, the aura of the ending of the land, where at the far tip you look out towards America 3,000 miles away. The hill ridge and watershed runs parallel to the northern coast with the longer streams flowing southwards. This is the quietest route, the climber's route to Land's End.

The first hill at the eastern end is Trencrom with its ancient camp. The land is now so narrow that the view from most high places extends from the northern to the southern sea, where the

great pile of St Michael's Mount is always conspicuous. Trink
Hill is next, then Rosewall Hill over against the coast road; a gap
at Towednack is followed by Trendrine Hill. Of these moors
Andrews wrote:

> There is a stillness on the moor which is unique. When there is a
> wind you feel it rather than hear it, as there are no trees to take the
> place of the harp's strings. When the air is still there are many
> small noises, the rustling of bracken or of blades of grass, or the
> movement of some small animal in the undergrowth that is only
> noticed when hearing is sharpened to pick up infinitesimal sounds,
> just as the eye is for objects that at first it can hardly see in a
> dull light. It seems as if distant sounds were blanketed by an
> invisible barrier on these uplands where you seldom hear the sea.
> Though a bare land it has a beauty of its own.

The line of the ridge swings inland with Zennor Hill thrusting
northwards from it towards the coast. Much of this belongs to the
National Trust. Rocky tors rise here and there but none big enough
to provide more than a few feet of climbing. The cromlech on
Zennor Hill has partially collapsed. A south-easterly spur terminates in Castle an Dinas, with an Iron Age fort, and nearby is
the well-preserved Iron Age village of Chysauster. The Penzance
to Gurnard's Head road is crossed between Mulfra Hill, with its
cromlech—Mulfra Quoit, and Bosporthennis where there is a
prehistoric beehive type hut.

The next stretch of moorland, at present the wildest of all, is
threatened with the reopening of the tin mining using open-cast
methods which would make a modern industrial landscape in the
place of the overgrown ruins of an ancient one which we see
today. The coast road runs on a broad shelf at around 400 ft, a

———

(above) Rosemergy Ridge, near Bosigran. Climbers have reached
the top of one of the pillars of this easy ridge; (below) Granite
Cliffs, Isles of Scilly. Fine coasteering terrain near Peninnis
Head, St Mary's, hardly explored so far

raised beach above which a former cliff line rises steeply to 700-800 ft. In spite of their modest height, Hannibal's Carn and Carn Galva with their rocky slopes and tors might well be mountains of much greater stature. The summits look out across the northern sea. Half a mile away, Watchcroft at 826 ft is the highest point of West Penwith. Southwards stretches a wide moor broken by the upstanding chimney of Ding Dong Mine, which slumbers quietly on a day of sunshine but is eerie, almost frightening, in mist and rain. First worked by the Romans or perhaps even earlier, who knows how long before it will be teeming with life and work again. On this moor also are the cromlech, Lanyon Quoit, now restored and preserved, the inscribed stone of the 5th or 6th century—Mên Scryfa, and the curious holed stone of Mên an Tol. It is easy to creep through the hole and you will never be the same again.

The moor beyond the Morvah road is dominated by Chûn Castle, a fort on a hill top, even though the hills further south are somewhat higher. Carn Kenidjack, another small rocky tor, is prominent on the hills above Botallack. Andrews says of it:

> Its loneliness in close proximity to the populated centres of the tin mines is perhaps the cause of the legends that have grown up round it, for though the old superstition that centres round haunted places has largely disappeared in Cornwall, it dies hard. Even today the natives like company when they cross desolate tracts of moor at night.

Remains of mining arise on every side, engine houses, chimneys and occasionally a fearsome unprotected shaft, which just goes down into the darkness.

(above) The Steeple, South Devon. An unclimbed foreshore pinnacle immediately east of Soar Mill Cove; (below) Vixen Tor, Dartmoor. The long side on which there are a number of harder routes. The 'highly polished cleft' of the ordinary ascent is on the far side

As the land continues to narrow the ridge runs southwards to Bartinney Down, below which at Carn Euny is an interesting fogou, or ancient underground chamber. Chapel Carn Brea, 657 ft, by analogy with other 'last' features hereabouts may perhaps be called the last hill in England. The sea lies all around now and from here the cliffs and rocks are largely hidden so that the fields appear to run to the water's edge. The summit is spoilt for the moment by the unsightly remains of some Second World War defence works, nevertheless this, with all the hills and mountains of England at one's back, is emphatically 'somewhere' in much the same way as Land's End.

THE COAST

The former coastguard path can be traced most of the way round West Penwith, and this will probably be the line of the S-W P C Path, a total of about thirty miles. It follows the strip of rough land between the edge of cultivation and the cliff top and from its very purpose overlooks the sea whenever possible. We begin at St Ives of the painters, a gay little holiday town of narrow streets and wide sands; we pass round Porthmeor Beach and aim for Clodgy Point, the first headland to feel the full force of the Atlantic. For the next few miles the raised beach is prominent along the top of the present-day cliffs. The road westwards from St Ives runs at the back of this, skirting the slopes of the old cliff line and leaving a wide area untouched near the sea's edge. As far as Carnelloe there are in fact two routes here—the cliff path close to the edge, and the field path further inland linking the line of farms which runs along the raised beach platform. The latter gives a quiet uncluttered view of the rich local wild life, the former is likely to be of more interest to the coasteer. The granite does not appear before Wicca Pool and is not continuous until beyond Porthmeor; the cliffs at first are killas and greenstone. A cliff foot traverse is straightforward, though slow maybe, all the way to Halldrine near Bosigran Head and there are numerous easy ways down. Mine chimneys soar up at intervals, becoming more plentiful as we move westwards. For the first few miles there are coves with sands and the cliffs are not specially high. There is a fine stony beach at Treveal with a natural bath for swimming, while offshore the seals gather to sun themselves on the Carracks.

Wicca Pillar, a sixty ft granite column, is the outstanding feature of the next cove. There are climbs, too exposed for the non-climber though easy enough; the problem of access from the field path down slopes covered with vegetation and boulders provides perhaps more serious difficulty than the climbing. Trilley Rock, offshore, has been reached by swimming.

The next out-jutting point is the slate and greenstone Zennor Head; its broad bulk is bounded on the east by the sandy Porthzennor Cove, from which a fishing boat used to operate in the last century. On the far side is Pendour Cove where the line of the S-W P C Path has been indicated now for many years by a signboard giving the gradient down to the Cove as 1 in 2. Off the next headland is Carnelloe Island, which has been reached by swimming. The cliff top route from here to the outstanding promontory of Gurnard's Head is tough going on account of the prolific vegetation. On the east side of the Head are two sandy beaches, on the other a small cove with a large foreshore pinnacle— Pedn Kei. Half a mile on is Porthmeor Cove, with a fine natural pool and from here granite continues unbroken to Pendeen Lighthouse. The tiny Halldrine Cove, where there is a small crag in quite delectable surroundings, leads on to the great 400 ft headland of Bosigran below the rocky hillside of Carn Galva. There are mine ruins and the West Country headquarters of the Climbers' Club—Bosigran Count House—is only a few hundred yards of quaggy scrubland from the cliff edge. We slope across towards the stream which runs down into Porthmoina Cove to reveal the finest rock scenery of this northern coast. Below Bosigran Head, on the east of the Cove, is the colossal granite crag known as Bosigran Face, the upper half of which, above a grass covered horizontal ledge, is nearly all verticals and overhangs. The western wall of the Cove is a pinnacled Alpine-type ridge with granite towers rising one above the other from the sea's edge to the cliff top; this, since the Second World War, has been called Commando Ridge, though for the previous fifty years it had been Bosigran Ridge. Between these ramparts in the centre of the Cove is a substantial foreshore islet, variously called Bosigran Pinnacle, Porthmoina Island or the Battleship. In fact it looks more like a cocked hat, having steep walls on either side with easy angled ridges towards land and sea.

Pendeen Lighthouse is about three miles ahead. The cliff top gives rough going at present with vegetation, boulders and small rock faces; the slopes are steep and little can be seen from near at hand of the traverses along the sea's edge made by A. W. Andrews in the early years of the century. We pass Morvah, with its prominent church and a mine chimney, on the cliff and so reach the sands of Portheras Cove, where climbers send their families to swim and make sand castles. One of the best known of the fogous—Pendeen Vau—is on the cliff above, while the church at nearby Pendeen is modelled on the Cathedral of Iona. Between here and Cape Cornwall is the mining coast of metamorphosed rocks; industrial relics surround us on every hand and the traveller must keep a wary eye open for tottering walls and unprotected shafts. Geevor Mine is still in operation; further on is the Levant Mine, which penetrated to 2,000 ft below sea level and half a mile out to sea. The workings at Botallack were on ledges on the cliff face; here too the tunnels were driven out under the sea, and it is said that on stormy days the miners could hear the rocks on the sea bottom rolling about over their heads. Half a mile off Cape Cornwall, which has its own personal mine chimney, are the Brisons (ninety and seventy-one ft) which can be reached by a powerful swimmer. Michael Drayton noted them in *Polyolbion*:

> Upon the utmost end of Cornwall's furrowing beak,
> Where Bressan from the land the tilting waves doth break.

Defoe believed mistakenly that the mineral bearing ores cemented together the strong rocks of this coastline and thus helped them to resist attack by the sea; in fact the metalliferous strata are often easily eroded leaving behind those steep-sided clefts, which are known as zawns in this party of the country. Henceforward the cliffs are lower, backing eventually the broad sands of Whitesand Bay. At the southern end, sheltered under the headland of Pedn Mên Du, granite once again, is Sennen Cove, a delightful small resort and climbing centre. A pleasant cliff top path leads on to Land's End.

Very many visitors have come to Land's End and many of them have written about it. What is there to add? It is probably the most popular place of pilgrimage in the West Country and is very often overcrowded. Early in the morning or late in the evening, on days of storm or in mid-winter, something of the magic of the ancient Bolerium, or Pedn an Laaz, can still be sensed in

spite of the hotel, the cafés and the car parks. The climber below
the cliff's edge sees the best of it, missing even these. It is, then,
unmistakably somewhere important—the seas of Britain stream-
ing out on either side behind, the 3,000 miles of ocean ahead. In
fact the majority of visitors are content to reach Dr Johnson's
Head beside the hotel and only a proportion attain the real Land's
End, which is Dr Syntax's Head beyond the First and Last
House.

The castellated granite cliffs, now at their finest, stay with us
along this south coast, almost to Lamorna. The first seven miles,
says the *Thorough Guide*, and many will agree with it, 'are considered
to equal if not to exceed in grandeur and beauty of cliff scenery
any other of equal length in these islands'. At the first headland—
Pordenack Point—two fine ridges run from sea level to cliff top,
one with a series of sharp spires, the other with a prominent perched
block, the Helmet. We can look back now, from much less
crowded surroundings, on much the same view as from Land's
End. A mile and a half away Longships Lighthouse is the sign-
post at the cross-roads for the mariner; closer in are the ridged
offshore islet of the Armed Knight and the bulky foreshore mass
of Enys Dodnan. The *Thorough Guide* says, in a manner most enterprising for a tourist guidebook, that the latter may be 'reached at
low tide by those equal to an awkward bit of crag work.' They
find that there is in fact an arch on the outer side, through which
a fine view of the Armed Knight is obtained. The next headlands
on our way are the twins Carn Sperm and Carn Boel, in a cove
nearby is a disintegrating pinnacle called the Diamond Horse, with
a notice-board prohibiting climbing! It looks unattractive and
unlikely. The sands of Nanjizel, or Mill Bay, follow. The turreted
promontory of Carn Lês Boel walls the opposite side of the bay.
The pattern of craggy headlands with more or less inaccessible
coves between continues for some distance; the rock scenery at
Carn Barra (Ardensaweth Cliff) and around Folly Cove is outstanding. Along these cliffs the going is much more straightforward than that of the north coast and the absence of a need for
'bush whacking' helps considerably with the appreciation of the
scenery.

Ahead now is Tol Pedn Penwith, the 'holed headland', named for
a great funnel hole on the far side, which in the usual pattern
plunges down to sea level in awesome precipices. The seaward

face of the cliff is formed by a series of five great bastions, among the finest climbing crags and the most striking granite scenery in West Penwith. From west to east climbers call these Bulging Wall, Chair Ladder, which juts forward and is prominent in the view from the west, Wolf Buttress, Bishop Buttress and Runnel Stone Buttress. A good view of the eastern end of the face can be had by descending to sea level past the funnel hole. On the top is a look-out and two conical shipping landmarks, which are in line with the reef of the Runnel Stone and its whistling buoy, a mile offshore. Seven miles out is the lighthouse on Wolf Rock. A short distance on along the coast is Hella Point, a conical promontory with perched blocks; round the corner low cliffs lead to the fishing village of Porthgwarra.

Half a mile ahead, past St Levan Church and the open air theatre of Minack, are the delightful sands of Porthcurno, accessible by road. The promontory of Treryn Dinas looms in front and in between is Pedn y Vounder, a small beach approached by a steep path, ideal for the family climber as the crags rise direct from the sand. On Treryn Dinas is the most famous of the Logan Rocks; the story of its upsetting and re-erection by Lt Goldsmith, RN in the last century is too well known to bear repetition. The incentive for this act of vandalism may have been sheer boredom or may have come from challenging accounts like that of the *New British Traveller*:

> Castle Treryn consists of three piles of rocks. On the west side of the middle pile, near the top, lies a logan, or moving stone, of a prodigious size, so evenly poised that a child may make it move, notwithstanding which the extremities of its base are such a distance from each other, and so well secured, that it seems impossible for any human force, assisted by all the mechanical powers, to remove it from its present situation.

The Logan does not rock now, but it is a wonderful place with plenty of easy scrambling. After Penberth Cove, the coast is wilder and less visited and the cliff path, up to now so straightforward, ultimately vanishes. There are a few rocks at Porthguarnon, while further on Tater Dû has a greenstone crag and a new automatic lighthouse, operated from Penzance seven miles away. Next come the valley and cove of Lamorna, made famous by artists, then the tiny port of Mousehole, where at Penlee Point the North Cornwall section of the S-W P C Path will terminate,

135 miles from Marsland Mouth. Roads lead on into Penzance town, where the Path begins its next section at the Albert Pier.

THE CLIMBING

Among Victorian mountaineers the names of Leslie Stephen, John Tyndall and E. F. H. Bradby have been associated at one time or another with this far end of the West Country. Stephen, who lived for some years at St Ives and was a prodigious walker on the moors, is said to have climbed on one occasion 'gangling and prehensile' up a chimney on Gurnard's Head. Bearing in mind the outlook of Alpine climbers towards any sort of rock in Britain at this time, there is little likelihood that he saw any connection between this and the Alpine mountaineering with which he was familiar. Tyndall travelled a great deal among British mountains, but usually only as a walker. Of Bradby even less is known, though much later on Haskett Smith credited him with an intimate knowledge of the sea cliffs around Land's End.

The history of local climbing began, though no one realised it at the time, with the purchase of the house known as the Eagle's Nest on the north coast near Zennor by Professor John Westlake, QC in 1873. Family visitors during subsequent years included a young newphew, who later on was to play a big part in the story. Arthur Westlake Andrews, born at Eastbourne in 1867, was brought up at Teffont Evias in Wiltshire where his father was rector. Here he developed his future climbing abilities by climbing trees, while in due course he became a champion tennis player and athlete. He represented Oxford at the high jump, won a gold medal in the mile in the European championships in 1893 and one year reached the semi-finals of the men's singles at Wimbledon. He climbed in North Wales, in the Alps and in Norway but it was not until 1902 that he began to influence the climbing story in the west.

In the meantime Haskett Smith reported in his book: 'To the true-souled climber, who can enjoy a tough bit of rock, even if it is only fifty, aye, or twenty ft high, the coast of Cornwall with its worn granite cliffs and bays has much to offer.'

It seems unlikely, however, that he did any climbing here at this time and there is no record that anyone else, except perhaps Bradby, took up his challenge, so that when Andrews finally did so in 1902 the rocks were still everywhere virgin.

The earliest climbs were made with his sister at Wicca, below Eagle's Nest, and at Bosigran; at the same time they began work on his now famous traverses, passages of the foreshore nominally between high and low water marks, which are nowadays an established part of coasteering. The first account of Cornish climbing, covering the north coast of West Penwith only, appeared in the *Climbers' Club Journal* in 1905, with a wealth of detail of geology, birds, flowers, antiquities and general observation, which makes Andrews the *beau ideal* of the modern coasteer. For many years subsequently most visiting parties were organised by Andrews; Haskett Smith, who sometimes joined in, later wrote:

> For most of us to cling to a perpendicular cliff while the raging surf boils 150 ft beneath us is quite sufficiently exciting; but Andrews has had to relieve the tameness of it by inventing a novel gamble of his own. . . . His hobby is to pass round the cliffs below high water mark, which means that you are always racing against time and tide. It is a thrilling game, and the worst bunkers in it are the zawns. These zawns are great recesses with sheer, parallel walls and often a considerable depth of water. The accepted practice is to jump in and swim across; but can it be justified to a tender conscience? Can a man honestly claim to have climbed round the cliff if he had done part of the distance by water? If that is legitimate, why not go the whole way by boat. It must be left to the casuists to decide.
>
> On one such occasion our party included a brilliant lady climber. Our leader and his sister had already swum the inlet leading to a zawn and landed on a low reef on the other side, when without warning this lady dropped off plump into the sea. What was our astonishment on finding that she could not swim a stroke? That anyone who was not absolutely amphibious could have gone through two or three seasons of that sort of work was wholly incredible. Of course, the brother and sister were in the water again in a moment and towed the unfortunate girl across to the reef, while the rest of the party raced back round the head of the zawn and brought a rope down the face of the rocks to their assistance.

During this same period there are but few records of other visiting climbers, though Geoffrey Winthrop Young was one. A year or two before the 1914-18 War he came with George Mallory, later of Everest, but it was forty years before he wrote an account of the ridge of Carn Lês Boel which they climbed. They wore nothing but sandshoes, expecting to meet no one except perhaps 'a smuggler, wrecker or pirate':

It was a rock surface of volatile changes, from chimney or column, crystallised, friable and prickly, to a sea- and time-smoothed perpendicular or overhang. We made the most of it, and of the fair weather, keeping conscientiously to the outside edge; and where the juts higher up gave back in easier alternatives, we chose the more steeply tilted slabs and cracks. The slow waves as we climbed into the sun muttered and yawned round the bases of the ridge, and the echoes whispering up the hollows in the walls met the ceaseless sibilant recession of broken water off the rocks.

J. M. Littlewood began an independent development of the cliffs round Chair Ladder and Logan Rock, but surprisingly enough his parties never met any of the others and it was not until after the first guidebook in 1950 that any co-ordination of the various efforts took place. During the 1930s Andrews wrote another series of descriptive articles for the *Climbers' Club Journal*, including the first accounts of Chair Ladder and Carn Lês Boel and the first mention of entrancing localities like Blinker's Bed, B's Bath and Green Cormorant Ledge. However, not many people came until the Climbers' Club acquired Bosigran Count House as a local headquarters in 1938. Colin Kirkus, probably the greatest rock climber of his generation, was one of the early visitors, but he made no startling contributions. It has been said of another famous climbing area—'our foremost experts seem to become so absorbed in the charm of their surroundings as to neglect the more austere aspects of rock climbing in a surrender to the joyous holiday spirit', and in those days this sentiment applied equally to the delightful surroundings of West Cornwall.

The Second World War was a setback for the rising popularity of the local cliffs. During the next few years the Commandos trained at St Ives; they had their own methods, such as grappling irons for some sorts of terrain, and used their own names for climbs. Indeed one of the most pleasant ridges in the Bosigran area, which had for nearly half a century been called Bosigran Ridge was renamed by them—Commando Ridge—and a commemorative plaque was in due course affixed thereon.

The most popular of the Commando crags was Pedn Mên Du at Sennen Cove and the rocks now bear marks of the heavy traffic on the holds of the most frequented routes. Hereabouts there took place a remarkable escape described by Frank Smythe in the *Alpine Journal* in 1946. Part of the training of these troops was to learn the art of falling, from that great exponent A. W. Bridge, and Commando Corporal Meddings owes his life to this teaching. During the course of an exercise a boat capsized at the foot of the cliffs. Hurrying to the rescue he slipped on steep grass at the cliff top, slid down and went over at a point about 100 ft high. He kept his head sufficiently to remember to jump at the last moment clear of all projections towards a rift at the base of the cliffs. The sea rising and falling in the rift was at its highest when he hit the water. Still alive, though with a dislocated shoulder, he at once seized a drowning man and after a struggle brought him to a ledge. Though recommended for a medal he did not get one, as his action was held to have arisen out of fortuitous circumstances.

Other climbers of established reputation came to Bosigran in the War years; outstanding among them that remarkable character, J. Menlove Edwards, who, it was said, 'was developing an amazing technique of getting out of rough seas on to near vertical rock'. 'Imagine trying to do this', adds the observer, 'with the waves breaking against the rock with such a force that they shoot upwards for thirty ft'. Even now, more than twenty years later, coasteers have not progressed to this scale of endeavour.

In 1947 a guidebook was decreed. Andrews was automatic choice for one author, I surprisingly was appointed as his assistant. Andrews knew his part so well that he had almost lost the ability to describe it for someone who had not been there before. We discovered, moreover, all the other things which had been going on—at Pedn Mên Du, Pordenack and Land's End—and had to bring them into line with the parts round Bosigran which were already known intimately. The result was a novel guidebook to a novel area and even though it has been criticised it did much to advance Cornish climbing towards the place it holds today. To Andrews it gave a quite unusual distinction. No less than forty-one years had elapsed since his previous and widely famous guidebook, written in collaboration with J. M. A. Thomson, to the great crag of Lliwedd in North Wales and this is a very long span indeed for the active life of a climber. Our Cornish guidebook, which appeared in 1950, was in fact very much in this older tradition. The specialist rock climbing part, which maintained in places a studied vagueness, leaving the reader some things to discover for himself, occupied only a part. The rest was about walking, birds, plants, antiquities, history, poetry and the sea—unusual ingredients for a modern climbing text. The standard of climbing achievement in West Penwith had thus, for various reasons, reached approximately that of British mountain rock climbing half a century earlier. The next fifty years of the development were accomplished here during the next decade, a stupendous rate of advance, so that by 1960 climbs were being done employing modern methods and techniques and comparable with the hardest in the land.

One of the crags profoundly affected was the huge Face at Bosigran. The 1950 guidebook had only described three routes here, though one of these—Zig Zag, VS, pioneered by C. J. W. Simpson in 1948—had already given a hint of what was to come. More than a dozen new climbs were added between 1955 and 1957, all of S to XS standard. On Chair Ladder, with a dozen climbs in 1950, around twenty more were made in the next decade. The rate of increase was most explosive on the cliffs at Land's End, where no less than nineteen new climbs were made during 1959. The tally was improved too by closer liaison with the Royal Marine Commandos and full details of their exploratory work at Pedn Mên Du, Chair Ladder and so on became available to climbers in general. An outstanding figure in all this original work has been J. H. Deacon of the Commandos, who had a hand in almost every new climb done at Land's End and Tater Dú, as well as making quite remarkable contributions at most of the other centres. Worthy contributions have come also from the Biven brothers, H. T. H. Peck, R. Goodier, V. N. Stevenson and M. B. McDermott. Standards are high now, yet in the latest guidebook the needs of the more modest climber have not been overlooked and careful instructions are included for numerous routes of more amiable standard.

The major crag areas are dealt with one by one in the following. At the same time it should be remembered that there are plenty of lower rocks in between, of lesser interest maybe, but very worthy for one reason or another. Some are quiet and secluded spots, where you will not meet either trippers or other climbers, some give interesting coasteering traverses, and so on, for this coast has something for us in every yard of its length. The climber with a car knows no limitations, the climber on foot, provided that he is so entitled, will probably use Bosigran Count House for the north facing coast and either Sennen or Porthcurno for the south facing. Though drinking water presents a problem there are many pleasant bivouac possibilities on secluded ledges tucked away on the cliff faces. Sennen is specially interesting for the visiting climber because M. B. McDermott of Peter's Cottage is a professional guide and under his expert leadership, and for the appropriate fee, it is possible to make any desired climbing expedition on any of the West Penwith cliffs, subject, of course, to a certain minimum standard of competence on the part of the guided. The modern climbers' guidebook is in two volumes—one for the north coast and one for the south and west.

As we move westwards, the first important crags are at Wicca Pool, approached from the field path near Tregerthen Farm over slopes with dense vegetation cover. It is an old-fashioned centre, opened up by A. W. Andrews years ago, where very little climbing is done nowadays and there are no climbs of particularly high standard. The chief feature is a granite pillar some sixty ft high, easily accessible from the cliff behind by a route of only D standard. Other harder ways can then be tackled with a rope from above. The granite makes only a fleeting appearance here and does not outcrop again until Porthmeor. Along the intervening coast there are many traverses, scrambles and short climbs on a variety of rocks, access problems to coves, and at least one large foreshore pinnacle at Pedn Kei, so that this adds up to an attractive area for the gentler forms of coasteering. Stern modern developments have taken place on the steep seaward face of Carn Gloose. Further on, Halldrine Cove is a particularly pleasant spot with a delightful crag of easy climbing suitable for novices.

The next major climbing area lies in and around Porthmoina Cove, the rapid development of which since 1950 has already been described. Bosigran Face, forming the east wall of the Cove, is broken at half height by a broad grass ledge—the upper portion of the cliff is the climbers' crag. The ledge is accessible down steep slopes at the landward end and by a scramble down an open gully at the seaward end. The easier climbs lie beyond this gully (Black Slab D) and near the landward end of the crag (Ledge Climb D). The massive overhangs and steep walls of the part between carry a complex network of extremely hard routes, about fifteen of them, which are for experts only. There are two girdle traverses at different levels, both long and hard, while a traverse of S standard has been done round the seaward end towards Halldrine.

Branching off left from the landward way to the ledge on

Bosigran Face down very steep slopes of grass and broken rock and descending the last few feet with more or less help from a stainless steel ring-bolt and iron chain permanently in position, it is possible to reach the boulder bridge on the beach opposite Porthmoina Island. This can be crossed at all but the highest tides. The first summit of the Island is reached by a scramble, but the topmost involves an exposed pitch, either by the facing crack or a traverse round to the left. The crest of the Island can be followed easily almost down to sea level at the far end, while the steep sides provide a variety of ascents and traverses at various levels.

The west side of the Cove is bounded by the pinnacled Commando Ridge (Bosigran Ridge), which gives a delightful climb of VD standard. The foot is reached by a scramble down steep vegetation-covered slopes beyond the ridge, reached by climbing across near the top or through a gap half way down. On the far side of these slopes the West Ridge gives another easy climb, but this one is cut off abruptly at around half the height of the cliff, the lower part dropping vertically to the Great Zawn and the sea. A. W. Andrews, who passed along here at sea level in the course of a coasteering traverse in 1923, predicted with remarkable foresight that this wall would one day be climbed:

> Above are the unclimbed cracks and ledges of the lower West Ridge. There are certainly large niches, where the shags and guillemots sit and the wall might be climbed if it were possible to connect them.

No one was found to agree with him until 1957 when J. H. Deacon led M. E. B. Banks by a route (XS and A2), which they called Green Cormorant Face. Later the same year Peter Biven and H. T. H. Peck did another route here, entirely artificial with seven successive overhangs, the finish forty ft out from the base! The shags resented their intrusion and Biven mentions in his account the additional hazard of these birds trying to bite the rope.

The most interesting of Andrews's cliff foot traverses were made along this coastline between Porthmoina Cove and Portheras Cove. The section in the neighbourhood of the Great Zawn, mentioned above, was perhaps the most difficult:

> In front is a small platform below the ledge of the Green Cormorant, so called from the untiring sentinel who resents intrusion above. A narrow rift has to be crossed which is, however, too wide to bridge at the mouth. Descend a square-cut cleft, back and knee,

as near to the cliff as possible and then work outwards, and at the sea end upwards, till the extended legs and arms form a bridge at the widest point. 'Happening' on a good fingerhold, swing on to the wall in front and draw up on to a small mantelshelf. There is a good belay on a knob of rock a little above. A doubled rope must be used to reach the Great Zawn, as the wall has practically no holds for a few feet.

On the first visit Andrews had to build a pyramid of stones on the far side in order to escape. On the cliffs as far as Brandys Zawn there are some climbs at sea level and others on the higher slopes, accessible at any time; after that we are left only with the traverses. While few of the present day climbing visitors bother with them, coasteers of the future will come to regard this as the cradle of their sport. Finally we come to Portheras, which has a fine sandy beach and, as cars have to stop some distance away, there are access problems for the general public. A nearby crag enables the climbing father to please all members of the family simultaneously. The granite stops at Pendeen and we have to pass the mining coastline of St Just and the wide sandy sweep of Whitesand Bay to Sennen for the next major climbing area.

This is beyond the village on the headland of Pedn Mên Du, which is surmounted by a coastguard look-out. From here an easy gully runs down in the direction of Land's End towards an offshore pinnacle called the Irish Lady. After a few feet, a terrace leading down to the right provides a start for many of the climbs; at the far end a short descent leads to a platform thirty ft above the sea which gives access to the remainder. Below half tide it is possible to traverse right round the headland to the sands of Sennen. There are about fifty routes of up to ninety ft covering the whole range of standards. This is a popular place for the Commandos and the holds on the 'trade routes' are as nail-scratched as those of a mountain crag.

The Land's End area is another which has seen remarkable expansion between the guidebooks—from three routes in 1950 to twenty-six in the latest volume. The climbs are situated between the Sennen side of Dr Syntax's Head and the Hotel Buttress below Dr Johnson's Head. The foot of the cliffs in some places has to be reached by climbs of D standard, in one by an abseil after which the climber is committed to a route of at least S standard in order to get up again. World's End Approach, west of First and Last

House, leads to seven routes; Abseil Point, 100 ft to the south, leads to six more. Beyond Dollar Rock a D climb called Dingo gives access to five climbs, and forty yds further south climbs on the so-called Longships Promontory are reached by descending Escape Route (D). Hotel Buttress, which presents no access problems, is south of a large cove where the Hotel outlet pipe emerges; climbs which have been made in this cove are not recommended. Lengths of climbs in this area vary from 50 ft to 120 ft, many are two pitches, a few longer. Standards vary over the range, but are mostly on the harder side.

Between Land's End and Chair Ladder there are crags on all the headlands—most of them have been subjected to vigorous attack by climbers during the last decade. First comes Pordenack Point, which has expanded from three routes to twelve, then the twin heads of Carn Sperm and Carn Boel, then Carn Lês Boel, where the earliest climbs were made by A. W. Andrews. Beyond Pendour Cove is Carn Barra, or Ardensaweth Cliff, a two tier cliff with climbs on the lower part, which has improved from mere mention to eleven routes since 1950, and this is followed by Fox Promontory, which has advanced similarly from nothing to a dozen routes and a girdle traverse. One of the criticisms of the new guidebook, which is altogether more determined and more businesslike than the old, lies in the neglect of the long routes for the moderate climber which can be found on some of these cliffs. The Helmet Ridge on Pordenack Point for example, the foot of which can be reached by the merely moderate Trough Route, gives a fine Alpine-type ridge climb of no more than D standard, which is a suitable expedition for a moderate or even novice party with a not too experienced leader. Similarly the Great Gully on Carn Barra is a fine natural line the whole height of the cliff, with about five pitches of D standard. The left hand side of the crag on Pordenack and much of Carns Boel and Sperm are similarly straightforward.

The series of buttresses, known collectively as Chair Ladder, on the headland of Tol Pedn Penwith give the most interesting and most varied climbing on this south facing coast. Here the 1950 guidebook was sadly out of line, both topography and history were in a confused state at the time and, though some measure of progress was made, a true understanding was not achieved until some years later. In particular the account was written with no knowledge of the work of J. M. Littlewood's parties before 1939 and of the later Royal Marine Commando contributions. Only a dozen routes were described, therefore, where the modern guidebook lists nearly forty. There are easy ways down which are only scrambles on either side of Zawn Rinny to the west of the crags, and by using them the moderate climber can reach the sea level ledges, accessible on the low water side of half tide, and climb up by the Western Chimneys, the Great Slab Route, the Cleft Route or East Chimney, all of which are only D standard. When the topography of the crag has been grasped, some of these can serve as routes of descent, of course, for climbers in search of harder things. The climbs on Wolf and Bishop Buttresses are harder, but Runnel Stone Buttress has some straightforward ways. There are two big girdle traverses, one surprisingly only of VD standard. The longest routes give more than 200 ft of climbing and all standards are represented. It is a major crag in every respect even though, since discoveries at Morwenstow and on Lundy, it no longer gives the longest climbs in the West Country.

In the following lines M. E. B. Banks describes a typical granite climb—one of the earlier routes on Bishop Buttress:

Now that we were well above the high water mark the granite changed from the cold slippery texture of the chimney to that rough fawn rock, mottled with lichen, which not only delighted the eye but offered a host of small but safe footholds to the jagged teeth of our tricouni-nailed boots. The line of weakness now went upwards and a little to the left. The holds were small and the first moves, as Jimmy led them, appeared slightly awkward, tending to push him off to the left. He led up for some fifteen ft on typical Very Difficult rock until he found a belay and called me on. The

Limestone on Berry Head. P. Littlejohn leading the second ascent of Barbican (XS) on the recently developed Old Redoubt Crag

rock was now sun-warmed, and I felt in fine fettle as I climbed up to join him, the granite unfolding before me like a dappled carpet. Two more short but equally commendable pitches brought us to a steep wall beneath a wide ledge. It was only about twelve ft high, but the holds were far fewer and smaller than hitherto, and covered with a dull green lichen. . . . I moved carefully to the right along a narrow ledge, prospecting for a way up. On coming to the most likely looking place I gardened as much lichen as I could, exposing a set of small rugosities. Moving very gingerly, with delicately balanced movements, I reached a point midway up the pitch. Between my feet, far below, I saw the rock pool, now diminished to the size of a bath-tub conveniently placed to catch me. The pounding of the surf had grown fainter in my ears. A long step, pondered well before it was made, a couple of tense moves upwards, and the wall was beaten.

A little further on are Porthgwarra Buttress and Hella Point, both with some climbs and on towards Porthcurno there are more pitches and problems. Pedn y Vounder, below Treen village, has a sandy beach reached by a steep path. There is a slab and a series of what might be termed typical North Welsh buttresses rising from the sand to the cliff top. They are straightforward, but have an air of going somewhere, while the family can be left below happily engaged in the normal beach pursuits. Logan Rock peninsula ahead has more than twenty pitches and short routes, which the guidebook leaves to the ingenuity of the visitor to discover. Beyond there are more odds and ends at various points—Cribba Head, for example, and Porthguarnon.

The last major crag is Tater Dû by Lamorna. Not even known to the writers of the 1950 guidebook, there are now seventeen climbs of all standards up to 160 ft long. The rock is not granite,

Limestone at Chudleigh. The climb is called Drip Dry and is entirely artificial. Most routes here are free climbs of the highest standards

H

but greenstone, such as we met in places on the north coast between Wicca and Halldrine. Probably the novice would do well to confine himself to granite at first, but the expert will find pleasant variety here.

THE SCILLY ISLES

The Scilly Isles, about 140 in number, are the summits of a granite mass similar to those we have already studied on the mainland. They lie some thirty miles south-west of Land's End. Only five are inhabited—St Mary's, the terminus of the steamer and helicopter services from Penzance, Tresco of the gardens, St Martin's, St Agnes and Bryher. There is a great deal of sand, and indeed St Mary's really consists of three islands united by sand dunes. The mystery land of Lyonesse lay between the Scillies and Cornwall, the story of its flooding being very similar to that of the Cantreff y Gwaelod in Cardigan Bay. The Seven Stones reefs are said to have been the site of a city in this vanished land. There are certainly signs of recent subsidence among the Scillies themselves—the seas are unusually shallow in places and it is sometimes possible to wade from some islands to others at low water.

The highest point is Telegraph Hill on St Mary's, around 160 ft, while St Martin's Head is only a few feet lower; there is thus no hill walking such as we have described in other parts of the West Country. The biggest island, St Mary's, is only some two by two and a half miles so that seldom, if ever, is the walker out of sight of the sea and all island travel is in fact coasteering. There is only one definite record of climbing, on Peninnis Head on St Mary's—this I will detail in due course. It seems likely however that a great deal of scrambling does exist on many of the islands and, with such a large number of relatively inaccessible rocks and islets, that part of coasteering which seeks to ascend little visited summits, and particularly where a boat is required for the approach, is remarkably well catered for in this magnificent rock archipelago.

There are three lighthouses, the first to greet the transatlantic traveller on his approach to Europe. The famous Bishop Rock Lighthouse, on what is very nearly the most westerly point of the islands is 160 ft high. Landing is no longer allowed, though at one time it was possible to be hauled from your boat to the set-off by a rope winch from the lighthouse, whence a ladder led vertically up to the doorway. The second lighthouse is on Peninnis Head, the third on Round Island on the north side of the group.

The rock scrambler on St Mary's will be attracted first and foremost to Peninnis Head where there is a chaos of granite boulders weathered into fantastic shapes. These include Tooth Rock, thirty ft high with a pointed tip, Monk's Cowl, Pulpit Rock, likened to the sounding board of a pulpit and fifty ft long, Witches Head, Giant's Foot, Sleeping Bear and so on, as well as those other formations typical of granite—rock basins of all sizes and stages of development and logan rocks, one of more than 300 tons. Near to Tooth Rock it is possible to reach a narrow ledge, known as Pitt's Parlour, above a sheer eighty ft cliff and it is here that the only recorded rock climbing was done a few years back. This was a traverse of extreme difficulty needing modern mechanised methods. The author of the account refers also to 'established climbing routes further along the coast', but it has not proved possible to contact him or obtain any idea of their whereabouts. There is a tremendous blow hole on the headland and a number of sea caves, one curiously termed Izzicumpucca; another, called Piper's Hole, is said to communicate with the better known hole of the same name on Tresco. There are noteworthy beaches and antiquarian remains on the island also.

The so-called Eastern Isles, consisting of a group of eleven small islands and numerous rocks and reefs, lie between St Mary's and St Martin's. None is inhabited at present though some show signs of one-time occupation, particularly Great Arthur where there was once a quay. They would provide possible and entertaining camp sites, if permission were obtainable. Great Ganilly is the largest island of the group, its area has remained unchanged for a century and a half. Great Arthur on the other hand, now only twelve acres, was formerly three times as large. The most interesting prospect for the coasteer would appear to be Hanjague, the most easterly rock of all, which rises steeply, turret-like, from deep water and might present an interesting problem of access and ascent. The hill on Great Ganilly, 110 ft, is the highest point hereabouts; this island is connected to that of Nornour by a series of reefs of flat rock like a pavement and to that of Great Innisvouls, at low water, by a slippery causeway of boulders which gives very hard going. Ragged Island, very rugged, is a bird island; Menawethan is also rocky and possibly worthy of exploration.

St Martin's, which occupies the north-east corner of the group, reaches 160 ft at its eastern end, where there is a red and white striped day-mark built in 1683 as a guide to shipping. The population, at present just over 100, has fluctuated widely in the past. This island is particularly rich in archaeological remains. The possibilities for climbing and traversing are unknown, though Kay writes of a 'shore indented by many bays and topped with great rocks, some of them piled almost perpendicularly and rising to an immense height' between Higher Town Bay and St Martin's Head. Offshore in places there are high rocks, such as Chimney Rock, while the north coast of the island is also wild and rugged, in Kay's words 'rock, grim and forbidding'. White Island, joined to St Martin's on the north by a low boulder bank, is rocky also, and here we find the third Piper's Hole of the Scillies. This one is situated on the eastern coast and may never have been completely explored.

The channel between St Martin's and Tresco is dotted with numbers of small islands, the most considerable of which are St Helen's, formerly St Elid's, and Tean, the size of which has diminished considerably during the last two centuries. St Helen's was inhabited long ago, for there are remains of a church and a monastic settlement; seen from here Baddeley describes Tean as looking like 'an immense cuttlefish, petrified and grass-grown.' Round Island, half a mile away to the north appeared 100 years ago to the Rev George Woodley as 'consisting wholly of rock, rising abruptly from the sea on every side, to a great height, and utterly inaccessible . . . its summit perfectly convex, its form round and its dark and lowering figure truly appalling.' It now supports the modern lighthouse, but landing is not allowed. Northwethel, says Kay, 'possesses some enormous rocks.' The Men a Vaur (Man of War) Rock is a pyramid divided into two blocks by a narrow chasm, which has, it is said, been traversed in a rowing boat.

Tresco, the second largest island, has extensive sands but little in the way of rocks. There is some antiquarian interest but the main features are the beautiful gardens, with plants from all over the world, the trees and the flowers. Cromwell's Castle, with its sixty ft tower, on the strait looking over to Bryher, was built in 1651 when the islands were finally occupied by Parliament; King Charles's Castle on the hill above was the last point in Britain to hold out for the King. The largest of the Piper's Holes is on Tresco, 200 yds east of Kettle Point. A sea cave some hundred yards long, it includes a small lake crossed by boat and terminates in a shingle beach. The granite walls, says Baddeley, 'crumble to the touch for a depth of a quarter of an inch.' There are other caves nearby, all of them may be part of ancient tin workings.

Only 300 yds west of Tresco across a shallow channel with a passage at very low tide is Bryher, the smallest of the inhabited islands. There are two summits, each nominally 138 ft—Watch Hill and Samson Hill. Shipman Head at the north end is a remarkable detached block of granite 130 ft high, separated from the main island by a channel some 10 ft wide and 160 ft long, and only accessible at low water. There are sands also, and a rugged west coast which looks out across numerous reefs and islets to the north-west—the Norrad Rocks. The most outstanding of these is the Scilly Rock, eighty ft high, which gives its name, though no one is quite certain why, to the whole group of islands. It is in two parts split by a chasm; here too there is a doubtful report of a traverse in a rowing boat. Gweal, near Bryher, is somewhat larger. Further south Illiswilgig is the biggest of a chain of islands running westwards from the tip of Bryher. Another, Castle Bryher, is sixty ft high. The chance of landing on these is likely to occur but seldom, or may not be possible at any time in some cases.

South of Bryher is Samson, the largest uninhabited island comprising two hills joined together by a low neck and extensive sands. Passage from Bryher is possible at low water, while it is said to be possible on occasions to wade from Tresco. There are numerous small islands around, Puffin and White Islands close at hand, Mincarlo away to the west sixty ft high and certainly accessible, and the Minaltos to the south—granite stacks not readily accessible.

Between Bishop Rock Lighthouse and the main inhabited islands are the so-called Western Rocks, large numbers of reefs, stacks and islets, among which navigation is extremely tricky. There are no beaches, but it is possible to jump ashore from a small boat in calm weather on many of them. All are the haunts of hosts of sea birds. First come Little and Great Crebawathen, then Rosevear, forty-seven ft high where the workmen lived while building the lighthouse; Rosevean, the highest at fifty-eight ft, Gorregan and Melledgan. This really is the outside edge of Europe. Annet, larger and comparatively flat, is maintained as a bird sanctuary and access is controlled. The great black-backed gulls with a wing span of several feet, are a serious menace to the smaller birds and will on occasions, it is said, attack a man. Offshore to the west are the Minmaneuths, otherwise 'the Dogs of Scilly and their Prey'.

St Agnes, at one time called St Warna, is the most westerly and the most southerly inhabited area of England. The lighthouse here is no longer used; in fact it was the misuse of this light which gave these islanders at one time the reputation of being the most unscrupulous wreckers in the West. The whole coast, says Kay, 'is nothing but a mass of rugged and practically inaccessible hunks of granite.' Lady Vyvyan, too, writes lyrically of the rock scenery of the south-west part of the island—'like some cyclopean sculptor's workshop, where half formed images of things never seen by human eye were piled rudely together or thrown carelessly aside.' The Punchbowl on Wingletang Down, consisting of a huge rock basin perched on an even larger rock needs, says Baddeley, a ladder for inspection; it no longer rocks, however, as it did in the 1750s. The Gugh, again with rocks and boulders in profusion, is an easterly projection cut off at high tide, which faces across St Mary's Sound to an almost identical feature on St Mary's called the Hugh. So we complete our anti-clockwise circuit of the islands, back to the departure point for the mainland.

For the coasteer the highlights would appear to be Hanjague, Peninnis Head, Men a Vaur, St Agnes, and Shipman Head; there are unlimited opportunities for cliff foot traverses and for the ascents of isolated rocks, pinnacles, islets, reefs etcetera. There are no points high enough to create a feeling of a hill or mountain background, yet there does exist some parallel with, perhaps even some extension of, that feeling we experience among mountains. As Lady Vyvyan says:

> Travellers in mountain country are aware of the diversity in form of any single peak as seen from one side or another and from one altitude or another. You become familiar in Scilly with the same changefulness in the islands' several forms. . . . There is, however, among these islands a more bewildering kind of changefulness than that noticeable in mountain country, and there are two contributory causes, the flatness of the sea and the movements of the tides. . . . The sea level base of all the islands lends to them a fantastic variety of form according to the standpoint of the spectator.

The rising and falling of the tides and the ever changing background of the sea multiply these sensations almost indefinitely.

5

SOUTH DEVON

DARTMOOR is the most easterly and the largest of the granite masses of the West Country; its summit, High Willhays, 2,038 ft, is the highest in England south of Kinder Scout. The Dartmoor National Park was designated in 1951 and has an area of 365 square miles, about half of which is high, wild and desolate moorland. That it is real mountain country can best be appreciated in the distant view from, say, the Haldon Hills or the high ground of North Devon; nearer at hand there are no peaks of striking outline to enhance the view, yet there is a real impression of massiveness and solidity. The interior has been likened to 'a sea after a storm suddenly arrested and turned to stone'; the *Thorough Guide*, on the other hand, dismisses it as 'one of the dullest and dreariest uplands of any extent in Britain.' The scale is big. From the edges of the Moor the traveller can look out over the plains, but in the centre of this extensive upland block he is cut off from the flat world outside. He experiences, in the words of one climber, 'that exhilarating sense of being on the roof of the world better than when standing on the summit of a high peak.'

There is wide variation in the colour of the local granite. As Baring Gould has written:

> Some granite is red as at Trowlesworthy, and the beautiful band that crosses the Tavy at Cleave; sometimes pink, as at Leather Tor; sometimes greenish, as above Okery Bridge; sometimes pure white, as at Mill Tor.

The tors are the striking feature of Dartmoor scenery. These weird piles of granite, often of grotesque shape and arranged in layers each having a rounded profile at the edges, sometimes form the actual summits of the hills, so that these can become inaccessible to all but the rock climber. There are typical examples at Great Links Tor, Great Staple Tor, Great Mis Tor, with its famous rock

133

basin, and the tourist haunted Hay Tor, where there are steps and some slight remains of a handrail. Others are situated on ridges, others, such as Vixen Tor, improbably nowhere in particular. Crossing estimated that there are 170 of them in the area. Relating the tors to the general scenery, Martin has written:

> It does not matter from what side the tors are approached because they will have an equal impressiveness. They take on the look of an almost guardian-like ring flanking the Forest; and to see them on a dark day in autumn or winter when mist hangs heavily over the carven summits where the hand of Nature has worked and moulded like a giant craftsman, is to get an impression of a grim enclosure protected at its edges by a fortress. On a summer day when the tors are glinting with a reflected light they are much more welcoming, like great entrances to a promised land of silence and seclusion.

Spread round the base of the tors, there is often a clitter, a pile of loose granite boulders torn from the crags by frost in some past glacial age. The finest examples are at Fur Tor, Great Mis Tor, Leather Tor and Hen Tor. The highest point, High Willhays, is overshadowed by its near neighbour, Yes Tor, which, though eight feet lower, is a much finer mountain with a rocky top and a fine view out to the north. The Atlantic, however, cannot be seen; it is hidden always by cliffs or coastal hills. These are the only points above 2,000 ft but there are several others, more widely spread, which are only slightly lower—Hangingstone Hill, 1,983 ft, Cut Hill, 1,980 ft, Great Links Tor, 1,924 ft and so on. Many of the other 170 tors are interesting from various points of view; we only have room for a few—Kes Tor, near Chagford, with the largest rock basin on the Moor, Bowerman's Nose, one of the most grotesque rocks, Ryder's Hill, 1,690 ft, the highest point on the southern Moor, Cawsand Beacon, highest point of the north-east corner, Crockern Tor, where the Stannary parliament used to meet, Sheep's Tor and Hound Tor, where there are fine climbable rocks, and North Hessary Tor with its controversial TV Mast.

This great hill mass is the source of many Devonshire rivers. For example, the Dart, as Camden tells us:

> . . . flows from the inner part of the County, and runs swiftly through certain dirty and mountainous places, thence called Dertmore, where Load-Stones have been found.

The other southern rivers, Avon, Erme, Yealm and Plym rise there, so do the Tavy in the west and the Teign in the east, while the north side gives birth to the Taw and the East and West Okements, both of which feed the Torridge. Yet on Dartmoor there are no natural lakes of any magnitude, since the ice sheets of the Ice Age did not reach this far south and there are thus no ice-worn rock basins such as we find further north in the country. Nowadays there are man-made reservoirs at Burrator, Holne, Fernworthy and above Shipley Bridge. The legendary Cranmere Pool, in the heart of the Moor at the head of the West Okement, has never held more than a trifling amount of water—indeed in dry summers it disappears altogether. Years ago just to reach it was a considerable feat and Crossing in his guidebook described routes to it from every side. A mail box was erected where visitors used to leave their own letters and collect earlier ones which they carried back to the valley for posting. A rubber stamp—'Cranmere Pool, Dartmoor, 1,825 ft'—available in the box, served to authenticate the process. This and a visitor's book are still there, but nowadays, unfortunately, the Pool is only a mile from Observation Point 15 on Okement Hill served by a metalled road through the Artillery Range from Okehampton and many more people make the trip. The immediate surroundings of the Pool, however, still out of sight of cars and road, will with any luck be found as wild as ever.

The heavy rainfall on a rock surface covered with spongy peat has produced large areas of bog all over the Moor. This usually takes the form of islands of peat and bog grass of widely varying sizes separated by channels of bare, black and soggy earth. Under any but the driest conditions this terrain provides very difficult going, involving constant casting around for fissures narrow enough to jump and on this account it is easy to lose one's sense of direction, particularly in the absence of prominent landmarks. Otherwise there is no very great danger, though from time to time it may be necessary to make a time-consuming detour. On the other hand the mires, called variously, 'feather beds', 'quakers' or 'Dartmoor stables', where the base is more liquid, can provide formidable obstacles. The most extensive mire areas, which should certainly be avoided, are between Cranmere Pool, Fur Tor and Cut Hill, though not of course on the higher ridges, the Raybarrow Pool area and the Red Lake, Aune Head and Fox Tor Mires beyond the Tavistock-Moretonhampstead road. A great deal has been written about the dangers of mist on the Moor, but a large scale map and a compass will go a long way towards minimising them. The lines selected should, wherever possible, avoid known areas of clitter or mire. In some places there is easier going in 'cuts' which have been made through the peat and provide passages suitable for men on horseback.

In former and more climatically favoured times, when the plains below Dartmoor were covered by a dense mantle of vegetation, the uplands, particularly on the south side, provided living space for large numbers of early people. Thus the Moor today is rich in antiquarian remains, of which there are several thousand consisting of hut circles, pounds, standing stones, stone rows and crosses, camps and burial chambers (cromlechs and kistvaens), enough to provide almost continuous interest for the walker. It has been estimated that about 1,500 hut circles can still be traced. There are remains of bee-hive type dwellings with a circular stone and turf wall at the base, formerly roofed by rushes or heather supported on poles. Pounds were walled enclosures round a number of such huts and included also sufficient space for cattle and sheep. The best known is Grimspound, north of Widecombe; there are others at Merrivale in the Walkham Valley, at Broadun in the East Dart valley and Legis Tor beside the Plym, while there are close groups of hut circles at Stanton Hill above Tavy Cleave and at Watern Oke nearby.

Standing stones, otherwise menhirs or longstones, stand either alone or in conjunction with stone rows. The most interesting are the Beardon Man, near Devil's Tor in the heart of the northern moor, a fourteen ft monolith at Drizzlecombe, east of Burrator Reservoir, and the Langstone on Cudlippton Down. The stone rows, or alignments, though not on the same scale as those at Carnac in Brittany, are outstanding in Britain. About sixty have been located hereabouts, the finest being that on Stall Moor in the Erme Valley, which is more than two miles long. There are more than ninety stone circles on the Moor some associated with barrows and other burial sites, others isolated and having a purpose unknown. The Grey Wethers on Sittaford Tor, the Scorhill Circle above the Teign Valley and the Dancers on Stall Moor are the best examples. The outstanding and best preserved cromlech is Spinster's Rock at Drewsteignton, but large numbers of kistvaens (a smaller version of the cromlech) and of burial cairns and barrows occur widely spread.

There are numerous ancient trackways and pack horse routes, to which we shall refer later when we come to discuss walking on the Moor. The pack horse routes crossed streams and small rivers by means of the so-called clapper bridges, large slabs of granite resting on granite piers, the best examples of which are at Two Bridges, Postbridge, Bellever and Dartmeet. The higher central portion of the area was the former Dartmoor Forest which was used for hunting by the Crown in mediaeval times. It later passed to the Duchy of Cornwall to which it still belongs. The lower moors round the Forest edges are common lands for the surrounding parishes which have certain rights over them and indeed over the Forest also.

All these western granite masses have been associated at one time or another with metalliferous mining and Dartmoor has had its share of this. It is uncertain when these activities began but the main period was roughly from late Norman to Elizabethan times. The industry was regulated by its own Stannary parliament which is supposed to have met, though it seems unlikely, on the summit of Crockern Tor by Two Bridges. At the beginning the tin was obtained either at or close to the surface; shaft mining began about 1500. From 1550 production began to fall off but continued spasmodically up to the present century. There was a brief revival of mining during the 19th century with copper the objective rather than tin and during the 1860s Devon and Cornwall together were producing half the world's supply of copper. The biggest concentration of mines is in the Tavistock area, where the search for various metals has continued off and on during the last fifty years. There are others closely west of Grimspound and at Birch Tor and Vitifer near Warren House Inn. Blowing houses where the ore was smelted can still be seen in places on the Moor; there are spoil heaps, shafts and ancient mine buildings but generally the devastation is not as bad or as widespread as it is in Cornwall. There is an unsightly china-clay works at Lee Moor over towards Plymouth.

There are three areas of indigenous woodland on the Moor, remnants of a much more extensive coverage, which are of particular interest—Wistman's Wood, beside the West Dart north of Two Bridges, Black Tor Copse, close to the West Okement below High Willhays and Piles Wood below Sharp Tor in the Erme Valley, Wistman's Wood, the best known, consists of a mass of stunted oak trees, ten to twelve ft high and at least 350 years old, which sprout from the boulders of a clitter; the trunks grow up and over the rocks, then down the other side giving a tangle of branches. Progress through the Wood is thus extremely difficult; so that, as L. A. Harvey tells us, 'although its estimated extent is only four acres it is safe to say that very few persons have traversed Wistman's Wood completely'.

Dartmoor has played only a minor part in the development of climbing in Britain. Haskett Smith, in his book, has plenty to say about it, but it is possible that his information came from his veteran friend, F. H. Bowring, who was a frequent visitor to Chagford. Haskett Smith wrote:

> It is curious rather than beautiful, and more interesting to the geologist, the antiquary, and the fisherman than it is to the mountaineer. Yet it is instructive even to him, for the frequency of rain and mist and the paucity of landmarks which can be seen more than a few yards off, coupled with the necessity of constantly watching the ground, render it one of the easiest places in the world in which to lose one's way in any but the finest weather. There are no true hills, but here and there a gradual rise of the ground is seen, with a lump or two of granite grotesquely planted on top of it. These are the Tors. As a rule they are very small, but often present problems to the climber, and are seldom without interest of some sort.

He also gave a list of the more prominent tors, but only half of them offer any serious climbs. At this time he had not heard of the Dewer Stone, but years later in a lecture to the Alpine Club he referred to the crag in glowing terms. His informant was H. Scott Tucker, a Plymouth member of the Club and an active Dartmoor walker, who incidentally had a hand in placing the original pillar box at Cranmere Pool. In later years, though few came to climb, the Moor attracted many a hard walker by its solitude and by the variety of things to be seen by the way. It was only after the Second World War that systematic exploration of the rocks took place.

All the National Parks in this country have their local difficulties and imperfections, often being forced to accept substantial divergences from the original principles on which they were founded. The clash between the preservation of natural beauty and the promotion of the enjoyment of that beauty by the public is always present, nor can we in our preservation yearnings afford to neglect the welfare of the local populace who naturally wish to have the same amenities of civilisation as the rest of us. The divergences from the original principles may involve the depressingly ugly re-afforestation of open hillsides, the impounding of lakes and valleys for domestic or industrial water supply, large scale commercial enterprises of various sorts and permanent military installations. Seldom are any schemes of this sort turned down when proposed for National Park territory in spite of the promises regarding the preservation of natural beauty implicit in the Act. The first two Dartmoor has suffered in small measure; the third is represented by the TV Mast on North Hessary Tor, an eye-sore which some folk find acceptable because it brings to the district the civilising influence of today's television programmes. It is, however, the fourth infliction which menaces Dartmoor most seriously and is in fact progressively destroying it as a scenic attraction or a centre for recreation.

The War Office first took over parts of the Moor as an artillery range in 1875 and by 1895 held about fifteen square miles south of Okehampton; the Willsworthy Range by Lydford was added in 1901. During the Second World War the whole Moor was taken over; so-called 'temporary' installations soon became permanent, such as a rifle range at Rippon Tor, hutted camps at Plaister Down and Bickleigh and a mast on Sharpitor. By 1947 the local authorities were compelled to agree to the permanent use of over sixty square miles by the military—an area very much in excess of that used before the War. Services encroachment continued, the Royal Marines taking over Ringmoor and Roborough Down in 1950. Not only is access to all these areas forbidden for much of the time, but the Moor is being disfigured by service roads, by indiscriminate building of hutments, observation posts, etcetera, by widespread use of live ammunition which is left around to menace the safety of travellers, by the wilful destruction of antiquities, by the driving across the moorland of tracked vehicles and by large scale camping. The last three of these atrocities are not confined, as one might have hoped, to the Services' areas, big as they are, but extend in fact over much of the National Park, simply because the military ignore their obligations in an arbitrary and irresponsible fashion. Every country lover, whatever his interest in the countryside, should do his utmost to reconcile the various interests which have to share the Moor. The visitor should not expect preservation to be carried to a point where obvious amenities of civilisation are denied to those living around, or should be prepared to pay on a national scale so that preservation and amenities can exist simultaneously. Each interest has to behave in a fashion tolerable to the others. It may well be that the military activities could be transferred to North East Scotland, but in the meantime they should be confined within the areas already demarcated for them.

The climber or walker must familiarise himself with the whereabouts of the various ranges and combat areas and the arrangements for indicating whether or not they are in use—usually red flags by day and red lights at night. Information can be obtained from local police stations or post offices. He must walk warily everywhere to avoid stepping on a bomb or tumbling into a rubbish pit or mortar hole; he must be prepared for a degree of desecration of trackways, ancient monuments and of the clean hillsides. He needs to be equally wary, says a local military man, of stepping on many tons of milk bottles and filthy rubbish left behind by visitors.

Perhaps the most ambitious expedition for the walker is a traverse of the Moor from Okehampton or Belstone in the north to Ivybridge or South Brent in the south and, as the railways from Exeter and Plymouth at present serve both ends, it is reasonably possible to come from a distance and do the trip in one day. It is about thirty-five miles, divided in two by the main road across the centre of the Moor. The Army roads at the Okehampton end make this part somewhat easier than before, but even so it remains a worthy undertaking and must have been done on numerous occasions. One such, probably not by any means the first, was carried out solo by Keith Lawder in the summer of 1911. He travelled by early train from Plymouth to Cornwood and struck due north by compass (in those days maps were a luxury and he did not have one). He passed eventually east of Princetown and followed the Cowsic River. Years later he wrote of it:

> My most vivid memory was that when in a swampy valley, walking on sedgy ground that moved underfoot, there was suddenly a bang overhead and a shell burst above me. The next thing was that I kicked my foot against an exploded shrapnel case. Being in a dip I could not see where the firing came from but I guessed the north so turned west to get off the range. In a few hundred yards I came on a row of head and shoulder targets facing west, and came to the conclusion that I might just as well continue in my proper

direction to the northward. Several more rounds burst overhead, but I was glad to observe they were progressively more behind me, evidently coming from an howitzer. Eventually in a lane leading off the Moor I came to the gun and it was indeed firing at fair elevation right over the route I had been following. The gun crew were shaken when I appeared and asked where I had come from; when I said I had just walked from Cornwood their faces showed polite disbelief!

He finished at Okehampton and caught a train back to Devonport. A crossing by J. H. Entwistle is described in the *Rucksack Club Journal* of 1923. He went from Belstone by Cawsand Beacon, walking as high as possible to avoid the mires:

. . . numerous clumps of reeds lie so close together as to conceal any suggestion of water, and even in broad daylight one's steps may imperceptibly become impeded by viscous slime, which seemingly rests on an unstable base, and which the apparently solid ground just a yard ahead hides with equally alluring effect.

Late in the day on the south side of the Moor he found the topography complex and the terrain trackless, but eventually by way of Harford Church succeeded in catching the last train from Ivybridge.

In the mid 1930s Keith Lawder repeated the trip with a companion in the reverse direction. They spent the night at Okehampton and, leaving at 8 am, not under fire this time, went by Yes Tor, Cranmere Pool, Cut Hill, Rough Tor, Two Bridges, Tor Royal, Yellowmead, and Ringmoor Down to the Dewer Stone. They finished a very long day by walking back from here to Devonport along the road.

Dartmoor lends itself to this kind of cross-country route from side to side and from end to end; these need, however, a fine day and the indispensable aid of map and compass, and are subject to local cessation of military activity and avoidance on the ground of areas of bog and mire. In the northern section, for example, pleasant walks could be made from Gidleigh to Lydford, from Okehampton to Postbridge and so on. The route from Postbridge to Lydford is the line of the ancient Lich Way, by which centuries ago corpses were conveyed to the latter parish church for burial; it is still haunted. East to west crossings of the southern section also give fine expeditions. An example is the Abbot's Way, which may perhaps have connected the Abbey at Buckfast with those of Tavistock and Buckland. W. G. Hoskins calls it 'one of the most solitary and most satisfying walks on the Moor, far from any of the summer crowds and the motor coaches.' The Abbot's Way runs round the headwaters of the Avon, the Erme and the Plym, while further north the Sandy Way sets off westwards from Holne to disappear in the middle of the moors. Dartmeet to Cornwood, South Brent to Yelverton, there are many promising lines; the One Inch OS Map shows miles of ancient trackway which might help the traveller on his way or, just as likely, prove completely elusive on the ground. But he will never be short of something to beguile the way. In the Official Guidebook to the Dartmoor National Park two moorland routes are described—in the north Gidleigh to Cranmere Pool by way of Scorhill Circle, Watern Tor and Hanging-stone Hill, six miles, returning by Okement Hill, the col between Steeperton and Wild Tors and Ruelake Pit, seven miles; and in the south, Princetown to Cornwood by Combeshead Tor and Shell Top, thirteen miles.

Beyond the western edge of the Moor, north of Tavistock, is the isolated Brent Tor, not granite but volcanic, 'a core of black rock rising out of a sea of grassland' to 1,130 ft. The tower of the church of St Michael on the summit is a landmark, in the (erroneous) words of the *New British Traveller*—'though twenty miles from the sea, an excellent mark for seamen which greatly assists them in bringing their ships into the harbour of Plymouth.' The ascent, which can be made by road for most of the way, is well worth the trouble for the extensive views towards Cornwall and indeed in every direction.

The Haldon Hills which separate the valleys of the Teign and the Exe to the south-west of Exeter are the most westerly outcrop

———

(above) Chalk Cliffs, Dorset. The great chalk headlands of Bat's Head and Swyre Head near Durdle Door, west of Lulworth Cove; *(below)* Durdle Door, Dorset. An arch in the Purbeck limestone which has provided a climb

of Cretaceous rocks in the country. Little Haldon, 811 ft, by Teignmouth has a golf course over the summit. The highest point of Great Haldon further north in woodlands is a few feet higher. There are too many roads for this to be good walking country but it has a fine outlook over towards Dartmoor.

THE COAST AND COASTAL CLIMBING

The S-W P C Path sets out on its South Devon journey from Turnchapel on the south side of the Cattewater at Plymouth. It crosses Mount Batten Point and follows the cliff top south and finally eastwards out of the Sound. Looking back we get our last view of this historic piece of England. Round the corner, half a mile off Wembury Point, is the Great Mew Stone, a craggy limestone islet a mile or so in circumference and 200 ft high, which more than a century ago had one occupied cottage. A mile to the east is the mouth of the River Yealm; close to the cliff edge in between stands the lonely church of Wembury. From Warren Point we cross to the south bank of the river by ferry. The six or seven miles of cliff between here and the River Erme show no trace of a cliff path at present, though it is proposed that the S-W P C Path shall eventually traverse this section except for a detour inland at Mothecombe. Near Stoke Point are the ruins of the old church of Revelstoke, further on St Anchorite's Tor, around thirty feet high, rises out of the furze. The River Erme is difficult to pass. Close to the mouth it can be waded with ease at low tide; about a mile upstream is a ford, but it is more than three miles to the first road crossing.

The Cliffs near Tilly Whim, Dorset. The climb is the very long Traverse of the Gods (VS) which leads from near Tilly Whim to the Sub Luminal Cliff

Beyond the estuary we come to high cliffs almost immediately; they reach over 300 ft at Beacon Point. Between here and Challaborough is a fine piece of coasteering country. Challaborough itself is an immense caravan town and is best quickly forgotten, but the two coves to the west, Ayrmer Cove and Westcombe Beach, are quiet; the rock scenery is good, and there are prospects of climbs both on the cliffs and on pinnacles on the foreshore. For many years we were intrigued by the magnificent-looking whitish rocks west of Hoist Point which appear from a distance to rise in great slabs. These looked specially promising in the view from Hope Cove and Bolt Tail, but when seen really close up they turned out to be far too steep for the quality of the rock; nevertheless it is a wonderful and unspoilt little cliff area.

Adjacent to Challaborough is Bigbury—popular seaside village. Page, writing in 1895 was a poor prophet (he should see it now!):

> Bigbury Bay is a lonesome place and, unless some enterprising personage thinks he can make a fortune out of the slate cliffs, is likely to remain lonesome to the end. . . . The district has probably altered little in the last hundred years, nor is the next century likely to effect much of a change.

Offshore is Borough (or Burgh) Island with its hotel, when cut off at high tide service is continued by strange stilted vehicles which run along the sands. The extensive sands continue past Thurlestone to Hope Cove, the cliff tops carry a number of large hotels. Out in the bay the Thurlestone Rock is a huge isolated sandstone arch, accessible at low water, said in some directions of the wind to roar loudly enough to be heard at Kingsbridge. I do not know whether it is easily climbable. Just short of Hope Cove there are two fine foreshore pinnacles which are unclimbed and an interesting looking slab on the main cliff above a small sandy beach, only recently ascended for the first time. One of these pinnacles looks difficult; indeed there is plenty of scope along this coastline for exploration at the present time. Hope Cove shelters behind the headland of Bolt Tail, from which there is a fine cliff top walk to Bolt Head, four miles to the south-east, along a continuous National Trust property. Whether a cliff foot traverse is possible is as yet untried. The rocks are schists with cracks and fissures in places crossing the path, so that Burton goes so far as to recommend that the walk should not be attempted except in full daylight. Halfway we pass the little cove of Sewer (or Soar) Mill, with a delightful small beach and the rocks of Priest and Clerk onshore; there are rocks, too, on the hillsides around, though not continuous enough for the climber. On the east side of the Cove is a cavern said to lead beneath the cliffs to Splat Cove at Salcombe—the legendary animal which entered this system in its natural colours and emerged white at the far end was no less than a bull! Half a mile on towards Bolt Head is Steeple Cove with a weirdly twisted foreshore pinnacle, about seventy ft high, unclimbed as yet and presenting a remarkably difficult problem. The summit of Bolt Head, over 400 ft high, looks across the Kingsbridge Estuary to Prawle Point three miles away. Plenty of rocks outcrop on the cliff tops and slopes hereabouts, yet none of them is sufficiently continuous to provide more than the briefest of scrambles. Our path runs high around Starehole Bay, past the grotesquely weathered rock ridges of Sharpitor and so down to Salcombe. There is a ferry to Portlemouth with another of Henry VIII's coastal defence castles. The church here has been mentioned as the scene of a famous incident from the days of wrecking. One Sunday during the sermon secret news was brought to the parson—he quickly ended his discourse, cast off his robes and dashed from the building shouting 'There's a ship ashore between Prawle and Pear Tree Point, but let's all start fair.' It was plunder not rescue which he had in mind. But the same story (and it is most unlikely in his case) is told also of R. S. Hawker, the Vicar of Morwenstow.

Prawle Point, the most southerly in Devon, is the next headland on this fine coastline, which Burton considers the equal of North Devon or North Cornwall. The cliffs are high and wild in the neighbourhood of Gammon Head, where two Spanish galleons went ashore and doubloons used to be found. The rocks here are still schists, which weather in a curious fashion, leaving behind the fretted shells of harder materials forming thin walls and edges. There may be just a possibility of rock climbing here and there and certainly access down the steep cliffs to some of the smaller coves would provide entertaining sport. Nothing is known of the cliff foot, largely because the working out of even a limited area may require preliminary large scale map work followed by considerable exploration by coasteers who are available continuously or very frequently. A Lloyd's Signal Station is sited on the Point, while at the extremity is an archway which can be traversed by boat in calm weather. Round the corner the coastguard path runs along an

undercliff with only low walls above the beach and rocky buttresses
—Nickleden Rock, Lobeatier Rock and others—jutting from the
hill slopes behind. There may be climbs.

At Lannacombe there is a small beach reached by motorists
who come by one of the most atrocious lanes in the county. It is a
pleasure to escape eastwards along the cliffs towards Matchcombe,
a mile ahead, which is only accessible on foot. Fantastic earth
pinnacles at the cliff's edge behind the beach are the striking
feature here, and there are pleasant sands. Only a short walk
remains now round Pear Tree Point—an abrupt turn in the coastline—to the celebrated Start Point, of which the alpinist T. G.
Bonney wrote—'rarely, except in the recesses of the Alps, have I
found a spot so perfect in its solitude or so impressive in its
grandeur.' There is a lighthouse and inland, 400 ft radio masts,
yet the headland retains much of the wildness which Page describes
in the view of it from the west:

> From where we stand it looks like nothing so much as a rocky
> skeleton, barely covered with a skin of turf. From vertebrae of rocky
> pinnacles, seamed and fissured by the storms of ages, ribs of rock
> protruding through the grass descend to the cliffs in lines curiously
> regular. The jagged tors—for such, indeed, they are—give to the
> headland a strangely weird appearance.

There is no climbing in the upper parts and no investigation has
been made of the lower, though it does not appear specially
difficult.

Start Bay stretches from here to the mouth of the Dart; there
is a shingle beach for most of the way and the cliffs are lower
and less resistant. After passing Hallsands (where coast erosion has
been accentuated in the past by removal of shingle) and Beesands,
each built right on the edge of the sea, the S-W P C Path reaches
at last the main road at Torcross, where it runs along the shingle
bank between the sea and Slapton Ley. This fascinating piece of
coastline, used incidentally to train American troops for the
Normandy landings in the Second World War, is of little interest
to the coasteer. For half a mile near Strete the path avoids the
road, but is soon back with it again through Blackpool (a contrast
with its mighty Lancashire namesake!) to Stoke Fleming. It then
follows the cliff, with several stacks below, round to Dartmouth.
The name of the last hill above the estuary—Gallant's Bower—
recalls a similar one far away at Clovelly.

There is a well-preserved coastal defence castle at Dartmouth; from here we cross by ferry to Kingswear where there is yet another. The coast east of the Dart, says Steers, is more remote and less spoiled than that to the west. It is grits and shales now, with outcrops of igneous rock—a colourful combination; we pass the Froward Points and on to Scabbacombe Head with Sharkham Point and Berry Head looming in front. Around Crabrock Point there are a number of small caves in the slates, while further on there are larger specimens in the Devonian limestone at St Mary's Bay. Below Durl Head is a large cave, while another running right through the headland near the Mew Stone can be traversed by boat. Now signs of civilisation begin to close in, for we are fast approaching the popular and prosperous coastline of Tor Bay, of which the 200 ft Berry Head, built in towering limestone, is the southern boundary. There are remains of a Roman encampment and of forts built much later in history to protect Brixham; there are some caves, a lighthouse and a look-out and, most important of all, some climbing crags. The original climbing area, pioneered by the Outward Bound School, runs for 400 yds from the tip of the headland to a point south-west of the Coastguard Station. For much of the length there is a ledge which makes it possible to traverse from one end to the other at all states of the tide. There are close on twenty routes of 50 to 200 ft, mostly of a high standard. The rock tends to be loose for the final thirty ft or so and, in fact, it is advisable to be careful everywhere. More recently a higher crag below the first fort on the headland has been explored; this is the Old Redoubt. The first route here, which gave 270 ft of hard climbing (XS), had to be reached by 300 ft of traversing also of very high standard. Then at Christmas 1967 came a 1,300 ft traverse topically named, The Magical Mystery Tour. Developments are taking place rapidly and it seems likely that the climbing here will turn out to be comparable with the hardest limestone in the country. A route has been done also in Freshwater Quarry down by Brixham Old Harbour, but climbing there is now prohibited. The view from the summit of the Head includes Dartmoor and the long coast of Lyme Bay—the red cliffs of Teignmouth and Dawlish, the high sandstone of Sidmouth, the first chalk cliffs at Beer and, close on fifty miles away, the limestone Isle of Portland.

The Path round Tor Bay will not be designated, passing as it does through the urban areas of Brixham, Paignton and Torquay, and it will restart at the south end of Babbacombe Bay. There are fine sands all along here. Except for the complex mixture of other rock types round Torquay itself, the red cliffs which begin near Paignton continue now to the River Exe and beyond. Some of the cliff features on this highly populated coastline are of great interest and a great deal of climbing exploration is going on there at the present time. There was a sandstone stack with an arch on the foreshore at Corbyn Head, and another arch in limestone is the so-called London Bridge. Nearby a number of new crags have been opened up by local climbers during 1967. Telegraph Hole Quarry has eight routes and Meadfoot Quarry six, while there are now more than a dozen climbs up to 200 ft on Daddyhole Cliff, which is a natural sea cliff. Shag Rock, Thatcher Stone and Oar Stone, a line of islets running from east to west, mark the side of a former river valley long since submerged. Hope's Nose is in limestone and half a mile further on the S-W P C Path begins again at Black Head, where the rock is a dark coloured basalt. To the north, Anstey's Cove has some fine climbing in limestone and there is a pinnacle which has been likened to a feudal keep. Long Quarry Point also has some routes. Then comes Oddicombe Beach, which is backed by sandstone but has headlands of limestone at either end; that to the north is Petit Tor Point, a grey crag scarred by quarries. Here too the current climbing expansion is proving very productive. On the beach beyond is a spiral rock of sandstone, Lot's Wife. At Watcombe is the picturesque Valley of Rocks with the famous Giant Rock; unfortunately for the climber these are all in a sandstone which is too soft to be of any use except perhaps on the rare occasions when it forms shore pinnacles. On past Maidencombe the cliffs continue high and bright red to the Ness at Shaldon, from which Teignmouth is reached by bridge or ferry. Eastwards, Brunel's railway, cutting off the sea from the land, protects the coastline from erosion but completely ruins it scenically. Only certain grotesque offshore pinnacles in the sandstone, such as the Parson and the Clerk, near Holcombe, are worthy of mention. The walker must follow the west bank of the River Exe to Starcross to find a ferry to Exmouth, by which he passes also into our next chapter.

CLIMBING INLAND

A. D. M. Cox gives a climber's view of Dartmoor in these words:

As regards climbing possibilities, Dartmoor may be said to provide almost unlimited climbing of a strictly limited type. That is to say, it possesses a great quantity of rock scattered at random over nearly its whole area, particularly on the summits of its hills, but this rock is only in very rare cases concentrated in cliffs of as much as 100 ft, and in those cases the steepness and peculiar formation of the rock do not encourage ascents. For the most part the climbing on Dartmoor is of the boulder type, but by looking for them it is possible to find many short routes which can be safely said to pass that nicely drawn line which distinguishes the mere boulder problem from the full-blooded one-pitch climb. The Dartmoor granite is of irreproachable quality and extremely rough in texture. Every mass of rock tends to be formed in bulging layers, each resting on the one below in the manner of the right-hand profile of the letter B. It will be easily understood that the climber who has attained a standing position on the lower curve is likely, particularly if he himself happens to bulge, to find his balance disturbed by the thrust of the upper layer in the pit of his stomach, and as a general rule he will find no handhold over the top to assist equilibrium. Roundedness, in fact, is the besetting vice of the Dartmoor rock. I recently came across a peak, presumably virgin, which was entirely round— an isolated rock some twelve or fifteen ft high, shaped like a football and absolutely without holds. The failing is most noticeable on the edges of cracks, which are usually not sufficiently clean-cut to do more than tantalise. At the same time it is not uncommon to find the rock cropping out into curious, illogical knobs and wrinkles and even 'jug-handles' which provide uniquely satisfying holds often where they are least expected.

Dartmoor climbing has no very well-ordered history. Haskett Smith, as we have said, listed some of the tors but as scenic features rather than as climbing crags. Vixen Tor, he says, 'is almost the only tor which has a distinct reputation as a climb.' It is ascended by a cleft to the surface of which, he goes on to say, 'the struggles of generations of climbers are said to have communicated a high polish'. However, it would appear that he himself had not seen it or done it, for there are no signs of polish nowadays, nor is any struggle needed. The Dewer Stone was discovered and some climbs made by H. Scott Tucker of Plymouth just after the turn of the century, but after this there are no records until the

1920s when D. G. Romanis and C. B. Jerram made some exploratory visits. Some ten years later A. D. M. Cox and his friends
pioneered a number of routes including two on the steepest part
of the Main Face. In 1948, members of the Royal Navy Ski &
Mountaineering Club, under the inspiration of Keith Lawder, began
systematic exploration. They found no trace of previous ascents,
much of the rock being covered with vegetation which had to be
cleared away before climbing became possible. Now a co-ordinated
body of knowledge began to grow and a typescript guidebook,
Some Rock Climbs near Plymouth by J. Derry was published
in 1950, with the first accounts of Dewer Stone, close on forty
routes; Sheep's Tor, sixteen routes; and Vixen Tor, six routes;
and brief mention of Combs Head Tor, the Staple Tors and
Leather Tor.

On the east side of the Moor, Hay Tor has long been attracting
tourists. 'Hay Tor', said Haskett Smith in 1894, 'was quite a nice
climb, but has been spoilt by artificial aids.' These, which took
the form of steps cut in the rock and a handrail (now cut down),
had already been in existence more than forty years. Back in 1851
a local writer had referred to:

> . . . the unsightly stair steps to enable the enervated and pingui-
> tudinous scions of humanity of this wonderful 19th century to gain
> its summit.

A. R. Thomson, a climber from the North Country, has described a
visit during the First World War, in which he made climbs on Hay
Tor, Hound Tor and Vixen Tor and on the pinnacle of Bowerman's
Nose, but here also detailed exploration did not begin until the
upsurge after the Second World War, when J. W. Denton, a
Torquay enthusiast, began to take a hand. His typescript guidebook
—*A Climbing Guide to Dartmoor*—included accounts of Hay
Tor, Hound Tor and Greator Rocks, Sharptor, Lustleigh Cleave
and West Mill Tor, about eighty routes in all.

Groups which have contributed to Devon climbing during recent
years have been the Commando Cliff Assault Wing, various Royal
Marine Commandos stationed from time to time at Bickleigh, and
the Outward Bound School at Ashburton, all of which use these
Dartmoor rocks in their training programmes. Many novices will
have begun their climbing careers hereabouts with one or other of
these. In 1957, when the first printed guidebook appeared, published

by the Royal Navy Ski & Mountaineering Club and edited by Keith Lawder, Devon had at last arrived as a climbing centre. We will now take a rather more detailed look at the various climbers' crags. The Dewer Stone, only eight miles from Plymouth, is by far the finest on Dartmoor, giving climbs of a mountain character of up to 200 ft. The situation is unusual, the Main Face, also known as the Devil's Rock, rising only a few feet from the River Plym, about half a mile up from its junction with the Meavy at Shaugh Bridge, in a buttress which juts out from a wooded hillside. The rocks far out-top the trees. In Baring Gould's *Book of Dartmoor* there is a picture of the rock drawn by E. A. Tozer. It would seem that at that time, the late 19th century, the surroundings were low bushes and small trees rather than the dense, high trees of today, for the rock towers in full view with distant scenery visible beyond. Left of Main Face is Main Gully followed by two subsidiary buttresses, Colonel's Arête and Pinnacle Buttress, with Mucky Gully between. From here a more or less level walk westwards leads to Penny Bay and a fifty ft pinnacle, the Tower. East of the Main Face and high up the hill are Needle and Raven Buttresses. There are other boulders and pinnacles around. 'The only objective dangers likely to be encountered on the climbs', says one account, 'are jackdaws and wet rock, both of which are prevalent in the Spring.'

On the Main Face there are some ten climbs of 150-220 ft of VS standard, though on the right hand side the so called Route B samples the steepness and exposure at a standard of only VD. From the upper reaches of the crag the climber looks out over a green sea of tree tops. There are short routes in and around Main Gully. Colonel's Arête, and Pinnacle Buttress give climbs of VD standard there are others shorter round and about, as well as a long girdle traverse across these and Main Face. Penny Bay has mostly problems of twenty to fifty ft, and it was on one of them that a well-known Devon climber had once to climb out of his trousers! Descending a rather tight tunnel, he became stuck and so climbed back upwards to get out again. Unluckily his trousers caught on a projection and, as the hole was too tight for him to free them, a companion had to descend and cut his braces at the shoulders. He was then able to climb out of his trousers and out of the hole. Needle Buttress gives a pleasant climb of 120 ft of VD standard, the Needle Arête, as well as some odd single pitch problems and a few recent routes of higher standard. Half way up the Raven Buttress is a prominent saddle, which can be reached by a scramble, by easy climbs or, if preferred, by ways even harder. The portion above the saddle gives routes of forty to ninety ft of varying standards. The river junction downstream from the cliff is a popular picnic place, but none of these casual visitors is likely to get thus far up the valley. The climber may well find himself, however, sharing the rocks with parties from Bickleigh or Ashburton.

Sheep's Tor, close to the village of that name immediately east of Burrator Reservoir, was explored by A. D. M. Cox in 1933. A forty ft wall of rock facing east is said to compare for height and appearance with parts of Harrison's Rocks in Sussex. It is a useful place for practice as a top rope can usually be arranged for more than twenty routes which are available, mostly of hard standard. This is another popular spot for picnics. Leather Tor to the north of the Reservoir has three climbs, while there is one also on a boulder 300 yds south of Combes Head Tor.

Vixen Tor, standing on the edge of a shelf on the moorland close to Merrivale Bridge, is said to resemble the Sphinx from some points of view. Because of this situation, the faces looking out on to the shelf are a mere thirty or forty ft high, but the steep south face dropping over the shelf edge is close on 100 ft. The ordinary route on the north side, Haskett Smith's 'highly polished cleft' (which turns out to be not particularly so) is easy, though a local man told Keith Lawder that visitors are occasionally stranded on the top afraid to descend and have to wait until ropes are brought from the quarry at Merrivale. There are easy climbs and scrambles on some of the surrounding boulders. The long face is a different proposition, having to the right a route of VD standard, which includes a stomach traverse along a deep horizontal cleft between two huge blocks, and further left other routes harder and steeper.

Hay Tor rises close to the Bovey Tracy–Widecombe-in-the-Moor road and there is likely to be the embarrassment of spectators in the summer, when cars and motor coaches stop by in large numbers. A big main block with a second, called by climbers the Low Man, away to the south-west gives a layout resembling Alms-cliff, the well-known Yorkshire crag. There are around thirty climbs on the two blocks, varying from short pitches to multi-pitch routes of 100 ft or more. Some particularly hard things have been added recently on the Low Man, including a girdle traverse of

190 ft. These again are popular with Outward Bound parties. Saddle Tor, beside the road somewhat nearer Widecombe has a few climbs and there are rocks and climbs also on Bell Tor, Chinkwell Tor and Honeybag Tor, which lie off to the north-west.

Hound Tor, one and a quarter miles north-north-west of Hay Tor, consists of perched blocks surmounting broken rocks sixty ft high. 'It derives its name', says Baring Gould, 'from the shape assumed by the blocks on the summit that have been weathered into forms resembling the heads of dogs peering over the natural battlements, and listening to hear the merry call of the horn.' There are three groups—the Hound Face, with two pronounced heads above the rocks, Perched Block to the west with nearby a tower called Top Hat, and behind Hound Face the Central Boulders and the Small Hat. On and around Hound Face are some ten climbs, a few of them multi-pitched of fifty to ninety ft with standards no higher than VD and prospects of harder variations. There are about the same number in the Perched Block area and still more on the Central Boulders. The topography is complex and a plan of the rocks is needed to understand it properly. Greator Rocks, a quarter of a mile to the south-east, also provide plenty of scrambling and some single pitch climbs of the easier standards. Bowerman's Nose on Hayne Down above Manaton is an isolated pinnacle giving a short climb of VD standard.

West Mill Tor, in the Artillery Range close to Okehampton, gives half a dozen climbs of twenty ft and a girdle traverse, first worked out by A. J. J. Moulam. The ascents of the topmost rocks of Great Links Tor, Great Mis Tor, the Staple Tors and Fur Tor need some degree of climbing skill and the summits of these particular hills are thus barred to the pure pedestrian. Eagle Rock, one and a half miles downstream from Dartmeet, has recently yielded some routes of sixty feet, while climbing is also reported at Bellever Tor near Two Bridges and at Bench Tor by Dartmeet. Some granite quarries on the Moor have also attracted attention; for example, there is one on the south side of the lakes in Leighon Valley near Hound Tor. Foggintor Quarry, one mile west of Princetown, has huge flat walls and corners of granite which would provide artificial climbs for anyone wishing to practise with pitons and étriers. Two have been done. Half a mile to the south-west is Sweltor (or King's Tor) Quarry, 100 ft high in the highest part; four climbs have been made and others await. This completes the tally of crags on the high moors and we now turn to various outcrops of a variety of rock types in the surrounding countryside.

Lustleigh Cleave faces south across the valley of the River Bovey above the village of Lustleigh. There is, says the guidebook enigmatically, 'every inducement for frolics, the place lending itself to summer picnics'; there are also half a dozen climbs of straightforward standards. The rocks, which are granite, comprise from west to east a pile of boulders capped by a loaf-shaped rock, a split pinnacle and a broken cliff with boulders above and below.

Two and a half miles away to the north-north-west is Blackingstone Rock which Mackintosh called 'one of the most striking granitic bosses in Europe.' Haskett Smith had this to say:

> A true tor, though not on Dartmoor. It is a fine piece of rock two miles east of Moretonhampstead. It is of loaf-like form, and gave a difficult climb until a staircase of solid and obtrusive construction was put there.

Several climbs have been made here in the last year or two. A mile away to the north-east is Heltor, which provides a further selection of ascents.

The rocks at Sharp Tor rise amongst wooded hillsides on the north bank of the Teign, one mile east of the Moretonhampstead–Okehampton road. There are West, Central and East buttresses of a slatey type rock separated by Great Gully and Intermediate Gully. These buttresses give straightforward climbs of D standard, on which, says the guidebook, 'much merit obtains in the negotiation of loose rock.' There are a few harder routes on the steeper walls above the gullies. Altogether it is a quiet and delightful spot. Some distance further down the Teign, about three miles short of Chudleigh, the dolerite Canonteign Rock, which is on private land, gives two climbs of 150 ft.

The Guide to Watering Places noticed the fine crag at Chudleigh:

> About half a mile from the town is Chudleigh Rock, according to Mr Polwhele, 'one of the most striking inland rocks in the island.' Viewed from the west, it is a bold and beautiful perpendicular object, apparently one solid mass of marble. . . . About midway down the cliff is a huge cavern.

The climbing history, which began only in 1960, shows a remarkably swift development up to the highest standards in the ensuing years, paralleling in fact the growth of limestone climbing in other parts of the country. Dr Tom Patey, then serving with the Royal Marines, was the first to realise the possibilities and the guidebook speaks of 'the awe-inspiring sight as this powerful climber hurled ivy and abuse into the surrounding air' during one of the original climbs. At that time the rock was almost entirely hidden by vegetation, giving climbs, as Peter Biven has written, of a 'Jack and the Beanstalk quality'; it has since been substantially uncovered. A typescript guidebook by F. E. R. Cannings and P. H. Biven appeared in December 1964, with a Supplement in October 1965 and an Addendum in April 1966. The rock is Devonian limestone and some at least has been a quarry at one time. There are two main walls—the South Face, with close on fifty routes, and the North Face with about thirty. The former is only 150 yds from A38 and is reached by a lane from Chudleigh Village, the latter forms the boundary wall of Rock House and permission to climb must be obtained therefrom. There are also a few odd boulders around. The South and North Faces are joined by an extensive cave system. Standards vary over the whole range, though the centre of gravity lies towards the higher end and only three of the climbs are D or M. Climbs range in length from 40 ft to 170 ft, some of the longer ones having three or more pitches. Each crag has a fairly lengthy girdle traverse. There is a shortage of natural belays and, when necessary, pitons, metal chocks and nut runners supply the lack. It is a fine addition to the climbing amenities of Devonshire.

To the west of Newton Abbot, Devonian limestone again provides climbing. White Rock, a quarry one and a half miles from the town, is close on 100 ft high, and there is another climbable quarry near Seale Hayne Agricultural College. There are routes also on a quarry-like cliff above the River Dart at Galmpton. Ausewell Rocks, one and a half miles north-west of Ashburton, once mentioned by L. S. Amery, do not seem to have anything to offer.

Morwell and Gunnislake Rocks rise impressively on the east bank of the Tamar between Morwellan and Gunnislake, and are well seen from the Cornish side from the long hill which runs down through the latter village to the border bridge. The first record of a visit was by C. B. Jerram and D. G. Romanis in the 1920s. Access is barred at the present time and we have lost, only temporarily let us hope, a very worthwhile crag. The material is a shale, less sound than the granite, and there is some vegetation. Seven main buttresses give routes of 100 ft or so, of which twenty or more were worked out a few years ago.

During 1965, some climbs of around 100 ft were put up in a limestone quarry between Turnchapel and Hooe Lake on the outskirts of Plymouth. These are mostly on the Hooe Face looking out towards the lake and are all of high standards. Round the corner to the right is Broken Gate Buttress; round the corner to the left is the Turnchapel Face, still carrying a considerable amount of vegetation. The rock is said to be substantially holdless, loose and unclimbable under wet conditions. It is private property. It is early yet to say exactly how important this will turn out to be, but it is certainly handy to Plymouth. A typescript guidebook published during 1965—*Interim Guide to the Climbing in the Plymouth Area* by B. Shackleton, describing this, also covers Sweltor (King's Tor) Quarry and the latest developments on Dewer Stone.

The climbs which have been done on the sea cliffs—the established and the new limestone crags on Berry Head, the recently discovered and rapidly expanding possibilities around Torquay, the older rock types between the Erme and Start Point—have been mentioned already in the Coast section. Considerable scope remains for development. The climbing visitor to this southern part of the country can intermingle trips to sea cliffs and to inland crags, as well as having access to the walking in the fine mountain area of Dartmoor, and these combine to give him as great a range of mountaineering and coasteering, of rock type and setting as he would find in a comparable area anywhere. There is an up-to-date guidebook, edited by R. D. Moulton, 1966, which gives full details of the routes at most of these places and where to find them. A guidebook to the climbing in Tor Bay is promised soon.

THE CAVES

The limestones of Devon are not as massive, neither are the strata as thick, nor the hills as high, as those of Somerset, so that this is a minor rather than a major caving area. Nevertheless, though the caves are less extensive, one or two make up for this by quite unusual complexity—for example there are some 4,000 ft of passages in Baker's Pit Cave at Buckfastleigh. Tough struggles, long verticals, stream passages and sumps are seldom found hereabouts and the opportunity for this type of caving is largely limited to old mine shafts and passages which, as in Cornwall, are being opened up again by experts. The scientific side of the sport, on the other hand, has received a considerable boost from the opening up of the Pengelly Cave Research Centre in Higher Kiln Quarry at Buckfastleigh in 1961.

The best known Devon cave is the famous Kent's Cavern in the Wellwood district of Torquay. It is a show cave with conducted tours along its one third of a mile of passages, which have electric light and artificial floors. The formations are beautiful. There is a museum on the site; the cave has also been a prolific source of antiquarian remains for numerous other museums further afield, as well as for that of the Torquay Natural History Society in Babbacombe Road. It has been called 'one of the oldest recognizable human dwellings in the country' and 'the British Museum among English caves.' Discoveries have ranged from the remains of flint implements, perhaps half a million years old, to spear heads, rings, and other objects of Roman times and later. Animal remains include those of various bears, mammoth, Irish elk, reindeer, sabre-toothed tiger, woolly rhinoceros and so on—an impressive list hardly equalled anywhere else in Britain. The first bones were discovered in 1824 and exploration continued under various hands until 1864, when a Committee of the British Association undertook the task on a thoroughly scientific basis. William Pengelly, a local antiquarian, played a prominent part in this work and afterwards described it by lecture and in print.

The biggest concentration of caves in the county is around Buckfastleigh, where the Devon Speleological Society have opened up more than a dozen during the last thirty years. No less than five of these are situated in the disused Higher Kiln Quarry, where the entrances were probably uncovered originally by the quarrymen; this was purchased in 1961 by the Society for the Promotion of Nature Reserves. Subsequently the Pengelly Cave Research Centre, named for the explorer of Kent's Cavern, was founded in the quarry for studies and research into all branches of cave science. Access to the five caves can only be obtained through the Centre; in due course tours will probably be organized in Reed's Cave, which is a complex with 2,200 ft of passages and has fine formations; Rift Cave, Spiders' Hole and Disappointment Cave, all much smaller, will be used for biological work; Joint Mitnor Cave with its rich hoard of mammalian remains has possibilities for excavation likely to be extremely rewarding.

Higher Kiln Quarry faces east on the hillside below Buckfastleigh Church. On the west side of the same hill is Baker's Pit Quarry, which has an extensive cave with 4,000 ft of passages. It connects with Reed's Cave, though the joining hole is too small to pass. Recently, the quarrymen at Bullycleaves, on the north side of the hill, broke into the Baker's Pit series, but the way is now closed again with quarry rubble. Many of the caves here are protected by the Nature Conservancy but *bona fide* explorers can obtain permission to enter Baker's Pit subject to the usual safeguards. The author of this book made a small contribution to the exploration of this particular cave, having assisted in the excavation of the so-called Dutch Oven Tunnel, which in the end, unfortunately did not penetrate to places new, but turned out to be an easier way into places already known. In the depths of the cave thus reached there used to be a Pyatt's Passage, which I was the first to explore, but again the honour was small, for the passage is in fact a very short ox-bow and returns in a pitifully short distance almost to the point where it started. I did experience here, however, the great excitement of digging for new caves—by far the most attractive side of the sport, at any rate for rock climbers. I learned also on the same occasion how careful cave explorers have to be, for going feet first down a passage which proved to be too narrow, I became wedged and had to be hauled out by my companions. Unaided I could not have moved. There are further caves in this district, mostly on private land; Rock House Quarry has a notable one 450 ft long.

A mile or so away, towards Ashburton, is the famous Pridhamsleigh Cave renowned, says the guidebook, for its reddish glutinous clay. Inside are 3,000 ft of passages, including in one place a narrow lake over 90 ft deep. Nearby is the shorter Little Pridhamsleigh Cave. There are a number of holes also round Chudleigh, where Chudleigh Cavern is 110 ft long and Pixies Hole reaches a depth of 100 ft. On Windmill Hill, above Brixham, a fine show cave is known variously as Windmill Hill Cave, Philp's Cavern and Brixham Cave. This also was excavated by Pengelly; flint implements, remains of cave lion and hyena and a reindeer antler were discovered. There are a few smaller caves on and around

Berry Head, at Cattedown, Plymouth, at Afton near Berry Pomeroy, and various other places.

During 1943 quarrying at Westleigh close to the Taunton–Exeter railway revealed a narrow fissure leading steeply downwards. Members of the Devon Speleological Society were invited to explore this and I was lucky enough to be asked to join them for the trip. The result was the interesting discovery of an almost vertical pothole, 110 ft deep; similar holes are common in Yorkshire, but rare in the West Country, though there is a sixty ft specimen at Bickington near Newton Abbot. Nowadays the supply of un-explored natural caves is running out in Devon and the ancient mine workings are attracting the attention of the ardent caver. It should be emphasised that this side of the sport requires the judgment of an expert, who must give meticulous attention to detail, and above all, to safety precautions.

6

DORSET AND EAST DEVON

THE HILLS

THE part of East Devon close to Exeter is not notably hilly, until we get beyond the River Otter and north-east of the Honiton–Cullompton road. In this area, which lies immediately south of the Blackdown Hills, between the valleys of the Culm and the Otter, North Hill near Broadhembury is 929 ft. There is a miniature plateau here above 800 ft, but as there are plenty of roads the most likely obstacles for hill walkers will be cultivated fields. Hackpen Hill, 845 ft, looks out over the Culm; from Dumpdon Hill with its fort, and St Cyres Hill above Honiton you can watch the cars on the A30 trunk road hurrying, when they can, ever westward. Between the Otter and the Axe the hills again reach 800 ft or so, while above Ottery St Mary a long straight scarp edge with a road along the top faces somewhat north-west. This rolling hill country, stretching up to Honiton and beyond, shelters Sidmouth from the north and provides it with a magnificent hinterland for short excursions and walks. Near Yarcombe, close to the Somerset border, the hills are again over 800 ft.

Most of Dorset is chalk country. The extensive chalk zone of Salisbury Plain was the centre of prehistoric England and the ridges which radiate from it were the main lines of communication to distant parts of the country. One of these stretches down into Dorset by way of Cranborne Chase and Bulbarrow Hill to Cerne Abbas, rounds Dorchester and, passing Maiden Castle, continues through the Isle of Purbeck to the sea at The Foreland (Handfast Point) near Swanage. The chalk is exposed elsewhere on the coast where the sea has broken through other rocks to lap against the side of the ridge. Westwards from Cerne Abbas the hilly country continues, marked by a line of ancient camps, to Pilsdon Pen, which at 908 ft is the highest point in the county, and on into Devon to the sea at Axmouth. This is not the sort of country to give long continuous walking lines. The following of ridge tops or scarp edges, often mixed up in a complex topography, is complicated by roads, cultivated fields and a lack of footpaths going in the right direction. It is likely that the hill walker will deal with it piecemeal; many fine short walking trips will be obvious from the contour lines on the One Inch OS map.

Cranborne Chase belongs in the main to Wiltshire, sweeping down from Salisbury to the Dorset border at Tollard Royal. Win Green Hill, 910 ft, the highest point of the Chase, is close to the border a mile or two away to the north-west. On the west side the hill mass terminates in a scarp edge above the valley of the Stour and the Blandford–Shaftesbury road. Shaftesbury, an ancient Saxon hill town, stands at 700 ft on the plateau edge and commands wide views over Blackmoor Vale. To the south, the River Stour flows through a gap in the chalk ridge below Hambledon and Hod Hills, both of which carry extensive earthworks, the former the scene of a minor battle in the Civil War, the latter having a Roman fort inside the perimeter. To the south-east of Cranborne Chase, beyond the Salisbury to Blandford Forum road, a wide and rather lower chalk area stretches towards Hampshire. The Dorset border in the north-east is the ancient Bokerley Ditch, raised by the Britons against the Saxons. Ackling Dyke, the Roman road from Salisbury to Dorchester, runs down through this countryside rich in antiquities to Badbury Rings, three tiers of defences on a conical hill, another of the great earthworks of the Stour valley. Opposite Hod and Hambledon, the hills soon rise again to 750 ft, the scarp edge facing north-west now. Bell Hill is 845 ft, and Bulbarrow Hill, 901 ft, has Rawlsbury Camp and the inevitable radio masts; nevertheless this section would make a fine walk. Complex hilly country continues past the Dorsetshire Gap, seamed with ancient trackways and conspicuous in the view from far off across Blackmoor Vale. Nettlecombe Tout and Ball Hill lead on towards Cerne Abbas and its famous giant. The huge, 180 ft chalk figure, carved on the hillside above the village is thought to be of Hercules and to date from the 2nd century AD. 'Glorying in his strength and advertising his virility', carrying a huge club, he is an art form very different from most other chalk figures. The ancient trackways, almost impossible to follow continuously in the modern age, continued across the valley of the Frome towards Eggardon Hill Camp which stands at over 800 ft above Powerstock. Eggardon, said Thomas Hardy, 'is one of the spots which suggest to a passerby that he is in the presence of a shape approaching the indestructible as nearly as any to be found on earth.'

The chalk ridge line returns eastwards now, passing south of Dorchester on the south side of the River Frome. A few miles along the way on Black Down the Hardy Monument (which commemorates Thomas Masterman, naval colleague of Lord Nelson, not the more modern and perhaps more illustrious plain Thomas) is only one of the fine viewpoints hereabouts, looking out towards the long line of Chesil Beach, with Portland looming beyond, and the coast from Devon to Purbeck. Three and a half miles east is Maiden Castle, the largest and best defended earthwork in the country; it has a 900 yds by 400 yds oval pattern, never less than three lines of ramparts and entrances ingeniously defended. The forty-six acres inside the banks, never ploughed even in the Great Wars of this century, have been undisturbed since the Romans left. It spreads across the downs, says Hardy, like 'an enormous many limbed organism of an antediluvian time—partaking of the cephalopod in shape—lying lifeless, and covered with a thin green cloth, which hides its substance while revealing its general contours.' Beyond the Dorchester to Weymouth road, which crosses at Ridgeway Hill, the hills are lower; there is a fine hill fort at Chalbury and a figure of George III on a horse is carved on the chalk slopes near Osmington. We look out from here across the busy bay of Weymouth to the Isle of Portland, Hardy's 'Gibraltar of Wessex', where the famous building stone is extensively quarried. The chalk reaches the sea and forms the cliffs at White Nothe and again at Worbarrow Bay. Hereabouts the Isle of Purbeck begins, with the Purbeck Hills running through it like a backbone, from Camden's 'steep and lofty mountain' of Flower's Barrow above Worbarrow, to Handfast Point by Swanage. This would make a fine ridge walk of about twelve miles, reaching to about 650 ft and passing the famous castle at Corfe on the way; unfortunately, at the present time the first mile or two at the Worbarrow end are in the military firing range and access is barred.

The ridge formed by the harder limestones of the Portland and Purbeck beds is lower and lies further south, so that it forms the sea cliffs for most of its length. Tyneham Cap, east of Worbarrow Tout is 549 ft and from here, starting in the military firing range, the ridge runs inland parallel to the chalk, reaching the coast again beyond Kimmeridge and terminating in the cliffs between St Aldhelm's Head and Durlston Head. This, too, is a great stone quarrying area; even in Defoe's time:

> . . . eminent for vast quarreys of stone, which is cut out flat, and used in London in great quantities for paving court-yards, alleys, avenues to houses, kitchins, foot-ways on the sides of high-streets, and the like. . . . There are also several rocks of very good marble, only that the veins in the stone are not black and white, as the Italian, but grey, red, and other colours.

Westwards from the neighbourhood of Cerne Abbas, Hippesley Cox traced a 'Ridgeway' over Batcombe Hill and on along the hills above the heads of the Rivers Yeo and Parrett, past Beaminster to the conical, wooded Lewesdon Hill, 893 ft, south of Broadwindsor. Pilsdon Pen, one and a half miles west, the highest point in the county, slopes steeply up from the valley. There is a capping of greensand and a hill-top fort. The next camp in the chain is Lambert's Castle above Marshwood Vale, where the ditches run round the 800 ft contour. The topography becomes complex, but the line of the trackway crosses the Beacon on Trinity Hill, between Axminster and Lyme Regis, passes Musbury Castle and terminates at the hill fort of Hawkesdon above Axmouth. The silting up of this harbour is of comparatively recent date and it may well have been an important port in these ancient times. This would hardly be attractive as a continuous walk, but the various hill tops and camps are of considerable interest.

THE COAST

Beyond the Exe the bright new red sandstone cliffs continue towards Budleigh Salterton. The S-W P C Path, starting again to the east of Exmouth, runs along the cliff edge. Beyond Straight Point the cliffs known as the Floors reach to over 400 ft and above them on the heathery West Down there was once a beacon and a signal station. It is less than a mile down to Budleigh Salterton, where the famous pebble beds in the red cliffs are of considerable interest to the collector. The general eastward drift of beach material along the Channel coast means that samples of these are often found much farther east—as far away even as Langley Point and Dungeness. The traveller by the Path has to cross the River

Otter and can then follow the cliff edge as far as Sidmouth. Leaving Budleigh Salterton, the cliffs are lower but after about two miles we come to Ladram Bay with a startling series of foreshore pinnacles in sandstone—at least half a dozen of them. The sand and shingle beach attracts large numbers of visitors, so that intending climbers, presuming that these rocks are climbable, would need to time their visit with great care. There are shallow caves also. We ascend now to over 500 ft on the impressive cliff of High Peak, which is the western portal of Sidmouth. This, says Page, 'is the most beautiful cliff in South Devon and it is also the loftiest.' The face of the cliff is very steep, though the rock is too soft to form a climbable crag; the view extends seawards from Portland Bill to Sharkham Point by Dartmouth. Filling the gap where the River Sid flows between High Peak and the equally high Salcombe Hill Cliff beyond, Sidmouth is one of the most charming resorts of the south coast. Our route follows the cliff edge eastwards over a series of 500 ft cliffs, separated by the steep-sided valleys at Salcombe Regis, Weston Combe and Branscombe, each of which enforces a descent almost to sea level. Between the first two, Ramshorn Rocks outcrop impressively on the cliff face, but they are not for climbers. Finally, at Beer Head we reach the first outcrop of chalk—the most westerly bastion of the 'white walls of England.' Much of this stretch of the coast can be traversed low down at all states of the tide.

The next few miles of coast are noted for the landslips which have occurred at various times during the last few centuries. There are planes of weakness where harder rocks—chalk, greensand, etcetera of the Cretaceous series—rest on clay rocks of the Jurassic series. From time to time the overlying rocks slide over these planes and subside on to the shore or into the sea. In March 1790 ten acres of cliff top slid seawards on Hooken Cliff close to Beer Head, dropping 250 ft or so in the process and forming the rocky mass of undercliff which remains a distinctive feature to this day. The village of Beer is in a cove between cliffs of chalk, which hereabouts outcrops in a somewhat harder form than usual. Inland on the road towards Branscombe are the famous Beer quarries, said to go back to Roman times. Stone from here was used in Exeter Cathedral 800 years ago. The workings are a complex system of tunnels, parts of which connected with the sea; it is possible to take a boat round to examine these openings, where contraband was once stored. Seaton occupies a wide bay at the mouth of the Axe, but almost immediately the high cliffs begin again leading on in a mile or two to the famous Dowland Cliff and Landslip.

The big slide took place here in 1839, when twenty acres of cliff top, having a mass estimated at eight million tons, subsided during Christmas night exposing a new inland cliff 200 ft high above a chaotic mass of undercliff, with pinnacles, small crags and the remains of the previous surface cultivation. Now there is a prolific tangle of self-sown trees and undergrowth threaded by a few paths; the whole area is a Nature Reserve—a unique laboratory for the study of self-sown vegetation. This type of scenery continues to the Devon border and on into Lyme Regis. The cliffs at Whitlands subsided in the usual pattern in 1765 and again in 1840, while there have been slides immediately west of Lyme Regis during the last decade. There are paths along all this broken cliff which the S-W P C Path will eventually use; occasionally there are rocks and pinnacles but as yet no thought of climbing. From Plymouth to the Dorset border the South Devon section of the path is ninety-three miles, while on ahead lie a further seventy-two miles comprising the Dorset section which terminates at South Haven Point at Studland on the south shore of Poole Harbour.

The neighbourhood of Lyme Regis is notable for fossils. Ammonites are the most common, large ones, it is said, to the west of the town and small ones to the east; even now, if you are lucky, you may still come upon bones or teeth of some huge reptile, many of which were discovered hereabouts during the last century. Looking eastwards towards Portland from the first summit of the Seaton road above Lyme Regis gives, says Whiteman, 'the best sea view in England . . . no two cliffs are the same colour'. In one place they are bright yellow, in another layered like a chocolate cake and in a third blue, almost black. This last is the lias clay which, when waterlogged, tends to cause the characteristic landslipping. The main road into the town falls 500 ft in less than a mile, while a steeper minor road leads down to the Cobb, the little harbour where the Duke of Monmouth landed, another good viewpoint for the cliff colours and scenery. Between Lyme Regis and Charmouth is the cliff called Black Ven. Part of the former coast road has disappeared in places and the edge can only be traversed on foot, the modern road makes a considerable detour inland. Hereabouts Hutchings, the 18th century local historian, described one of the steeper hills as 'Ye Plimlimon of Dorsetshire'; nowadays this would be regarded as more of an insult than a compliment. Beyond Charmouth is Stonebarrow Hill, followed by the 617 ft conical mass of the Golden Cap—the Six Inch OS Map calls it Golden Cup—which gets its name from the layers of greensand on the summit, a 'miniature Table Mountain'. The cliff path can easily be followed here; the beach has little to offer the coasteer as backshore is available all the way. Climbing is out of the question on such low grade material, in fact any cliff foot activity would be menaced by possible stone-falls. We descend from the Golden Cap to Seatown below Chideock and climb out again at once by Doghouse Hill to Thorncombe Beacon, 507 ft, which also has a capping of greensand, then down on the far side to Eype Mouth. West Bay is now a mile ahead along the top of West Cliff, nearly vertical, but only about 100 ft high. A small harbour has been constructed here at the mouth of the River Brit to serve Bridport. Sandstone cliffs continue for a further two miles by East Cliff and Burton Cliff to Burton Bradstock where the long curved line of Chesil Beach begins.

The Beach is a massive shingle bank stretching unbroken for fifteen miles to the Isle of Portland. After touching the coast for the first five and a half miles it becomes separated beyond Abbotsbury by a lake called the Fleet, which varies in width from 200 to 1,000 yds. The separation continues for eight miles to a point where the bank forms the connecting link between the Isle of Portland and the mainland; it finishes one and a half miles further on against the rock of the island. The Fleet outfalls into Portland Harbour at this end, bridged by road and railway at Small Mouth. The bank is both wider and higher, 600 ft by 42 ft, here than it is at Abbotsbury, 500 ft by 22 ft. A further curiosity is that the pebbles are graded for size, the largest to the south-east, the smallest to the north-west, so that you can, it is said, tell your position in a fog from size alone. This is a fierce place in a storm for the waves can sweep over the top; in one instance, a small boat was flung over. A completely satisfactory explanation of the formation of this unique Beach has not yet been put forward; the pebbles are local limestone and chert, flints, greensand, quartzite from Budleigh Salterton, jasper from the River Otter and granite from Cornwall, as well as others from even further afield.

After he has followed the footpath behind the Beach for the first two and a half miles out of Burton Bradstock, two alternative routes are open to the traveller on the S-W P C Path. From West Bexington, one of these climbs inland up Wears Hill behind Abbotsbury and follows the edge of the chalk downs, past the Hardy Monument on Black Down, across the Dorchester–Weymouth road, along the ridge above the White Horse, dropping to the coast again at Osmington Mills just west of Ringstead Bay. The second continues behind the Beach to Abbotsbury and its famous swannery and runs along the inland side of the Fleet to Weymouth; beyond Weymouth Bay the cliff top is followed to join the former route near Osmington Mills. However, the true coasteering route would appear to be the Beach itself. This presents the same sort of problem as a rock climb or a traverse of a steep-sided mountain ridge in that once the traveller has set out he has either to finish at the other end or return every step of the way he has come. True, in the eight miles beside the Fleet the OS Map shows three ferries, but the ferrymen are hardly likely to be on the look-out for customers from the far side, who must be rare indeed. The going would be tough and monotonous, though no more so than a Derbyshire moorland for example, but the surroundings and the solitude would provide ample recompense. The Beach plunges straight into deep water and bathing is not recommended.

Ahead of us is the Isle of Portland, 'lying on the sea', as Hardy says, 'like a great crouching animal tethered to the mainland'. It is a huge limestone block reaching to 424 ft, pear-shaped in plan, four miles long and one and three-quarters wide. Here is the source of the famous Portland Stone, discovered by Inigo Jones and used in the Banqueting Hall in Whitehall in the reign of James I and later by Sir Christopher Wren for St Paul's Cathedral; the United Nations Building in New York provides an up-to-date example of its continued popularity. There are tremendous exposures of bare rock on every hand left by the quarrying, while parts of the west coast are covered by stone shoots formed from the disposal of unwanted waste. There is an encircling cliff top walk of about eight miles. The highest cliffs are in the north but at Portland Bill, where the pinnacle of Pulpit Rock is noteworthy, they are less than fifty ft high. There is a lighthouse here and a small beach, while the Shambles Lightship lies four miles offshore. Half a mile away on the east coast is Cave, or Keeve's Hole, a blow-hole going down to sea level. The lower part, which communicates with the sea, is large enough to admit a small ship and it is recorded that in 1780 a forty-tonner was in fact driven inside. Fossils are plentiful; in places the rocks are composed almost entirely of masses of closely packed oysters.

In our coastal walk by one of the three routes described we have reached Ringstead Bay, where the National Trust has a sizeable holding of coastline. An interesting story of this bay concerns the so-called Burning Cliff, where in 1826 rapid oxidation of iron pyrites in the cliff face ignited oil-bearing shales which smouldered intermittently for the ensuing four years. A similar outbreak occurred nearly 100 years later. The eastern headland is the 500 ft White Nothe, the first big chalk cliff since Seaton. There is a zig-zag track here down to the shore. A mile beyond, close to West Bottom a 300 ft chalk buttress, known as the Fountain Rock, rises impressively, stratified horizontally with flint bands and seamed with long cracks. A shingle beach stretches from White Nothe for one and a half miles to Bat's Head, where the strata are vertical and there is an arch known as Bat's Hole, or 'The Eye of the Monster', spectacular when seen from the east at sunset. The main cliffs are of chalk with Swyre Head particularly impressive, but the bed of Portland Stone nearer the sea soon begins to produce distinctive features. The Cow and Calf Rocks, the Blind Cow and the Bull Rocks are remains of this wall, then at Durdle Door we reach a fine arch, forty ft high and wide, also in limestone. Close by there is a large caravan site! The outcrop continues through Man o' War Rock to Dungy Head. The cliffs behind St Oswold's Bay are of chalk, but at Dungy Head the chalk ridge rises to Hambury Tout behind the cliff line, which is all limestone for the next half mile to Lulworth Cove. An interesting feature along here is the Stair Hole, where the sea has breached the limestone outer face of the cliffs, but has as yet only made slight impressions on the softer beds behind. At Lulworth, on the other hand, the breach is wide; a considerable amount of the softer beds has been scoured away and the sea has reached back to the foot of the chalk ridge, forming the famous Cove— perfectly constructed by nature to suit the needs of man. There are several caves at Stair Hole including the Cathedral Cavern, where pillars of rock rising from the water appear to support the roof. In these various bays the pebbles are graded in an unusual way, the smallest at the sides, the largest in the middle. Below the cliff east of Lulworth Cove is the Fossil Forest, but it is not possible to continue very far in this direction because the cliff top is in military hands and, except for one path from Lulworth to Mupe Bay, is inaccessible for the next four or five miles. The S-W P C Path which has followed the cliff edge closely from Ringstead Bay is here forced to desert the coast altogether and to cross the army ranges from East Lulworth by a road which is only open part of the time.

The coastal section from which we are permanently excluded is, of course, very fine and interesting. The cliffs east of Lulworth are still limestone, while the chalk forms the ridge of Bindon Hill just inland. Within a mile is Worbarrow Bay; here, along a front of one and a half miles, the sea has broken through the limestone, which disappears at Mupe Rocks and reappears on the far side at Worbarrow Tout. The backing cliffs are all of chalk and reach to over 500 ft. Worbarrow Tout is a small, 100 ft promontory jutting out at the east corner of the bay, it is separated by a low neck from the main mass of the limestone ridge, which along Gad Cliff, half a mile further on, reaches a height of 480 ft. Tyneham Cap above Brandy Bay is the first summit on the ridge which now swings away from the coast. For the next four miles the cliffs are of kimmeridge clay. Access is possible to Kimmeridge, where our journey on the S-W P C Path can be continued. The cliffs in Kimmeridge Bay are vertical; further on the offshore Kimmeridge Ledges mark the outcrop of narrow limestone bands in the clay. There is a bituminous shale here, which would be used for fuel if it did not give off an unpleasant smell; oil from the shale is similarly useless for burning. Celia Fiennes, who toured the country near the end of the 17th century, noted that the poor people in Swanage burned stone with an offensive smell for both light and heat. The cliff top path continues to the fossiliferous cove of Chapman's Pool, a cliff foot route is also possible. The Pool is reached from inland by a toll road and from this it is a rough scramble down to the beach. The kimmeridge clay is still very much in evidence and gives the back of the cove a sombre look, however, the rocks are lighter coloured on the east side—the massive out-jutting headland of St Aldhelm (or St Alban). From this point, surmounted by a Norman chapel, there is a magnificent walk of about five miles to Durlston Head at Swanage. The path runs along the top of limestone cliffs often vertical, which have become an important rock climbing area. There are several quarries. At Winspit and at Seacombe for example, there are terraces on the cliff and subterranean cavities. Further on, the Tilly Whim Caves, very much a tourist attraction, are the result of quarrymen's work. Dancing Ledge, reached also by a trackway from Langton Matravers, is a break and a popular picnic spot; there is a lighthouse on Anvil Point. Durlston Head is really a part of the resort of Swanage; there are footpaths and cliff walks and here also we find the famous stone globe, which is ten feet in diameter and weighs forty tons.

The coastline changes direction abruptly from being parallel to the outcrops of the various rock types and proceeds to run at right angles to them. Swanage is sited where the softer rocks reach the coast and beyond it, to the north of Swanage Bay, we find the chalk once again. It ends at a promontory, The Foreland or Handfast Point, which points across Poole Bay to the Needles and the chalk ridge of the Isle of Wight, many miles ahead, with which it was once connected. The last of the Purbeck Hills is Ballard Down and this ends in Ballard Point, 382 ft, where the cliffs are vertical chalk. There are several features of interest to the coasteer between here and Handfast Point—pinnacles known as the Haystack and the Pinnacle, the caves of Parson's Barn and Little Barn, and finally off the point itself the chalk stacks of Old Harry, 58 ft high, and Old Harry's Wife of which only the base remains. Hardy described this spot in the *Hand of Ethelberta*:

> . . . windy, sousing, thwacking, basting, scourging Jack Ketch of a corner called Old Harry Point, which lay about midway along the track, and stood with its detached posts and stumps of white rock like a skeleton's lower jaw grinning at British navigation.

The S-W P C Path continues round Studland Bay to South Haven Point, where there is a ferry to Bournemouth. Since leaving Minehead we have come over 500 coastal miles through every type of seaboard scenery that England has to offer.

THE CLIMBING

The limestone cliffs of Dorset, from Swanage westwards, have one of the briefest climbing histories of any comparable crag area in the country. Though close enough to London to be visited at weekends, no climbing was done here during the 1930s or in the immediate post-War period, when the sandstone crags at Tunbridge Wells were being highly developed and climbers were even turning to chalk cliffs to extend the range of their activities. In 1960 I produced a gazetteer of British climbing crags—*Where to Climb in the British Isles*—which represented the state of knowledge up to mid 1959. It is interesting, in the light of the tremendous changes which have taken place since, to quote what I wrote about the county, as this was indeed the sum of the story at that time:

> There is some spectacular coast scenery but mostly in newer and softer rock formations. The possibility of a climb or two on the limestone on the west coast of the Isle of Portland, one mile north of Portland Bill, has been noted. Other sites in the county such as Durdle Door offer similar doubtful prospects.

In fact, the exploratory work was already well advanced, but was known only to the select few who were working on it, some members of the Southampton University Mountaineering Club and, independently, a group of climbers from London and Guildford. The first guidebook—*Limestone Climbs on the Dorset Coast* by B. M. Annette—was published later in the same year.

Twelve months later Dorset cliff climbing earned the unusual distinction of a full article in the *Alpine Journal,* an astonishing departure for a publication which is essentially devoted to mountains and gives very little space to Britain anyway. John Cleare, who made this breakthrough, painted an attractive picture of the new playground—'tier upon tier of yellow roofs split by fantastic diedres and chimneys', its background and its potentialities. The limestone here is different. In Avon Gorge and in Derbyshire the Mountain variety is grey, the Devonian limestone of Berry Head and Chudleigh is grey also, but the local Purbeck Stone rises in yellow walls which, says Cleare, 'are akin to the Dolomites, having more in common with the Cima Grande than the Avon Gorge.'

Many of the aspects of coasteering are available along this seaboard, although in the first five miles between Durlston Head and St Aldhelm's Head the prospects consist almost entirely of conventional rock climbing, requiring, however, unconventional means of access. The cliffs, which fall steeply into the sea, are formed in straight or gently curved lines and there are no major bays or indentations. There is no foreshore or backshore and the long traverses, of which there are several, are on flat block ledges and over boulders resting upon them. Unlike the Bristol Channel coast the tidal range here is small, in fact only about six feet, so that the limiting factor on climbing near the water is the height of the waves rather than of the tide. The guidebook divides the climbs into three types—sea level traverses, which are wave washed and have numerous holds in the form of chert nodules left where the limestone has been removed; single pitch climbs, often on walls resulting from quarrying, which end on a flat ledge also quarried so that there are no finishing problems; longer routes, which have a seriousness due to steepness and remoteness and, not being water washed, are open to some doubts with regard to the quality of the rock. There are in fact three distinct strata of limestone; the lowest has been described as the 'best limestone in the country', the quality of the second is comparable with that of ordinary Mountain Limestone, the top layer tends to be more loose though still not as bad as some limestones elsewhere, then come the slopes of mixed earth and rock! There are few easy ways down and many of the routes have to be reached by abseil from the cliff top, in which case the climber must have reasonable confidence that he can climb out again. In the early days, it is said, a climber was once forcibly rescued by the lifeboat when bivouacing at the foot of one of the walls. Between the top of the crags and the flat top of the cliff are steep and loose convex slopes which provide their own hazards. Cleare writes of the top of one of the climbs:

> I pulled up awkwardly on to a mantelshelf only to find myself kneeling with my nose against a crumbly wall of steep earth, invisible from below. Lobster-claw crampons might have helped, for I had to carve a dozen steps, and use my hammer-spike as a dagger before I could reach more level ground, and the fence-post belay.

He points out the impossibility of providing a rope or rope ladder to facilitate the exit because of the difficulty of identifying the tops of the climbs from the cliff edge. Indeed, it is very hard to get a look over at the rocks without becoming involved in quite serious rope tactics. A good mixture of free and mechanised techniques is required—certainly this is the nearest place to London where artificial climbing can be practised. A great many climbs remain to be done—'high crags which offer fantastic lines every few feet'—but let us hope that we shall not finish up with a guidebook which names, describes and classifies all such parallel ways.

Before writing about climbs it is necessary to add a word of warning. Limestone climbing is a specialised activity, for which practice climbing on other rock types is not necessarily an adequate introduction. The aspirant climber should work his way through routes of gradually increasing standards, learning about the vagaries of the rock from positions of comparative safety before trying conclusions with it in positions of potential danger. Thorough safeguarding is of course essential, while it is very dangerous to climb on some of the crags, or to attempt even the easy traverses, when the sea is at all rough. Bathing, says the guidebook, 'is exciting, but dangerous if one enters the water loaded with ironmongery'.

As most people will arrive first at the Swanage end of these cliffs we will begin the description there. The stretch below the grounds of Durlston Castle and on as far as Anvil Point is subject to certain access restrictions; in this connection an agreement has been reached with the Durlston Castle Company and particulars have been published by the British Mountaineering Council. It is very important for climbers to be aware of the details of this before making a visit. There are half a dozen climbs on Durlston Castle Cliff on Durlston Head and permission to climb must be obtained from the Manager of Durlston Castle on the day. Immediately beyond we come to Tilly Whim, an ex-quarry area where the public is charged admission to see the caves, part of the former workings, during the summer months. The chief feature here is the so-called Main Ledge, in the neighbourhood of which there are four separate crag faces. Eastward from the Ledge it is possible to traverse for about 300 ft past two natural arches to a cliff which provides some fine 100 ft routes. John Cleare's account of one of these, Rendezvous Manque, gives some idea of the nature of the climbing hereabouts:

> The first pitch follows a narrow rib petering out at a small stance in a niche. Above this a bulging crack, the crux, is climbed until a step left on to a steep slab can be made, above which all progress seems impossible, for now the whole cliff tilts out past the vertical. However, above the slab is a tiny hole. The climber crawls into it and belays. Further exploration into the heart of the mountain, in true Lockwood's Chimney style, reveals an upper chamber, leading up and out into the back of a chimney splitting the upper overhang. This is climbed in superb position, back and

foot, right out above the sea to the crest of the overhang, and so to the top, where the transition from steep rock to steep grass and earth presents little difficulty. The climb is not too hard, about severe, and is a perfect introduction to the big yellow walls of Dorset.

This cliff area is now known as Tilly Whim Sea Walls and is open during winter months only to members of recognised clubs who have obtained the previous permission of the Manager.

There are two rock faces at Tilly Whim above and below the Main Ledge, while a third looks west at the western end of the Ledge. Numerous routes were put up here in the early days, but under the recent agreement climbing is now strictly forbidden at all times. A long traverse, the VS Traverse of the Gods, giving about 2,000 feet of climbing and involving some fairly advanced rope techniques and a swim, starts near the west end of Tilly Whim. It runs below the Anvil Point Lighthouse and ends at the next cliff crag—the so-called Sub Luminal Cliff.

Here the horizontal starting ledge runs with occasional breaks, awkward to negotiate, along the whole length at some height above the sea, and more than thirty routes of around thirty-five ft have been made between this and the cliff top. The ledge is reached down one of the easier climbs; the rock is excellent, giving the most easily accessible and least serious climbing in the area. The section immediately beyond is known as Boulder Ruckle from the jumble of huge rocks at sea level, recalling the use of the same name for a similar feature in Eastwater Cavern on Mendip. The climbing here is first class, although there is a tendency for the routes to be similar in character, as one north country expert has said—'Once you have done a limestone HVS anywhere you have done them all everywhere.' The wall is 120 ft high and gives about thirty-five routes, including some of the most serious problems—Ashes and Diamonds, Marmolata, Tatra, Jericho Groove and others—in the Swanage area. There is, in fact, no straightforward approach of easy standard and it is usual to reach the foot by abseil. It is also possible to traverse from Sub-Luminal Cliff, from which a 400 yd route of S standard has been worked out, not a very serious undertaking under calm conditions but liable to be dangerous in any kind of sea.

Cattle troughs beside the path on the cliff top give a name to the next stretch of climbing. An almost continuous ledge, ten feet above the sea, gives access to more than forty routes of twenty to forty ft, mostly of easier standards, though a sprinkling of harder have been added recently. The next crag area rises above the Promenade, another prominent continuous ledge. The climbs of forty to sixty ft have to be reached by descending a route of D standard, or by abseil. There are awkward cliff foot traverses from here back to the Cattle Trough area and on to Fisherman's Ledge, the next to the west. This is a secluded spot sheltered by large overhangs; two routes have been described and others are possible. Blacker's Hole is reached by a path and there is an easy climb down to the cliff foot ledges. Guillemot Ledge, further on, is reached down a gully followed by a climb of D standard. There are several routes.

The next landmark is the Dancing Ledge which is easily accesible by a track from Langton Matravers and is a popular place for trippers. It has an area of about an acre and is just awash at high tide. There are numerous routes of twenty-five ft or so of all standards and this, like the Cattle Trough area, closely resembles the sort of outcrop crag climbed upon in other parts of Britain. There is scope for development on westwards from here. The next established climbing area is at Seacombe, where a twenty ft wall between two quarried ledges provides numerous routes of straight-forward stands; there is a long traverse also. At Winspit, a miners' track leads back east towards Seacombe; 200 yds along it there is a steep wall, followed by another 100 yds of ledge—Cormorant Ledge—which can also be reached from the cliff top. There are some possibilities, a few climbs have already been done. There are more prospects at the Rabbit Warren, 200 yds west of Winspit, and from just beyond here it is possible to traverse at the cliff foot as far as St Aldhelm's Head. Close by the east side of this headland there is a small crag with some sixty ft routes, which, though the rock is poor, have the advantage of accessibility when the sea is rough. The cliffs on the west looking into Chapman's Pool are too loose to be comfortably climbable. Cars can be brought, unfortunately, to this point along a track from Worth Matravers.

The most concentrated climbing and the best prospects for the future are in the five miles of cliff described above. However, ascents have been recorded in places elsewhere along the cliff line of the county. Between Chapman's Pool and Durdle Door there

L

has been no quarrying for limestone on the cliff faces, so that all craggy places are topped by slopes of earth and rocks. Where the crags are at all high there are overhangs and loose rock, but even so, long cliff foot traverses can still be worked out; for example, there is one of 350 ft round the base of Worbarrow Tout, at present inaccessible, and another close on a mile long between Lulworth Cove and Mupe Bay. This is nominally of D standard but can be both hard and dangerous under any but the best calm summer conditions. Immediately west of Lulworth Cove, on the seaward face of the cliffs below the Coastguard Look-out there is a crag of poor quality with three routes. A climb has been made at Stair Hole and a traverse most of the way from the Cove to the Hole. Yet another crag by Dungy Head has yielded routes and the traverse westwards from Stair Hole can be followed all the way to Man o' War Cove. There is one climb also at Durdle Door. 'Cliff Climbing is Dangerous' notice boards have been placed at a number of points hereabouts, expressing a sentiment with which even the hardened coasteer will be inclined to agree.

The west coast of the Isle of Portland has impressive cliffs, 100 ft high in places, with poor rock and steep loose material above. Nothing has been done so far, though a few short climbs have been recorded below Weston. On the east coast there is a promising fifty ft quarry one mile north of the Bill; there is plenty more rock about but no very good prospect of sport. At the Bill itself there is a foreshore pinnacle, the Pulpit Rock; a carved slab disclaims any responsibility for accidents to climbers. It gives one climb on the outer face; a leaning flake of rock gives an easy way on the inner.

Dorset chalk has received little attention so far from the climber. The various pinnacles off Ballard and Handfast Points would provide problems similar to those successfully overcome at the Needles and would require a boat and possibly some sort of rope projection. Old Harry himself, however, needed only a boat —the climbing was reported as not difficult, only harrowing. We know from the *Alpine Journal* that John Stogden practised hereabouts for his Alpine mountaineering more than 100 years ago, but there is no record of what he did—probably it was just glissading and step cutting rather than rock climbing. Where the chalk outcrops again far to the west at Beer one climb has been done but there are no details.

Cliff foot traverses may well be possible in other places below a variety of rock types—where there is a backshore these will be straightforward, elsewhere there may be coasteering problems. There are few foreshore pinnacles along this coast, the notable exception is Ladram Bay where there may be promising possibilities. The only account of climbing which remains is one inland site, the Agglestone, otherwise known as the Devil's Night Cap, a sandstone boulder fifteen ft high on Studland Heath to the north of Swanage. Seven climbs have been done with several variations, so that it is a pleasant spot to pass in the course of a country walk.

BIBLIOGRAPHY

GENERAL

Leland. *Itinerary.* Written 1534-43, published 1710

Camden. *Brittania.* Original in latin, 1586; translation into English by Philemon Holland, 1610; several subsequent translations

Drayton, M. *Polyolbion.* 1613-22

Defoe, D. *A Tour through Great Britain* 1724-26

Walpole, G. A. *New British Traveller* 1784

Anon. *Guide to Watering Places* Early 19th Century

MacIntosh, D., *The Scenery of England and Wales.* Longman, Green, 1869

Haskett Smith, W. P. *Climbing in the British Isles—England.* Longman, Green, 1894

Baddeley, M. J. B. and Ward, C. S. *Thorough Guide—South Devon and South Cornwall.* Dulau, 1903

Baddeley, M. J. B. and Ward, C. S. *Thorough Guide—North Devon and North Cornwall.* Dulau, 1908

Steers, J. A. *The Coastline of England and Wales.* Cambridge, 1947

CHAPTER 1. SOMERSET

Baker, E. A. and Balch, H. E. *The Netherworld of Mendip.* J. Baker, 1907

Harper, C. G. *The Somerset Coast.* Chapman & Hall, 1909.

Balch, H. E. *Mendip Caves.* 1948

Burton, S. H. *Exmoor.* Westaway, 1952

Coysh, A. W., Mason E. J. and Waite, V. *The Mendips.* Hale, 1956

Barrington, N. *The Caves of Mendip.* Dalesman, 1964

Dixon, J. *Limestone Climbs in South West England.* Limestone Climbing Group, 1964

Can Exmoor Survive? Exmoor Society, 1966

Ward Drummond, E. *Extremely Severe in Avon Gorge.* Privately, 1967

Johnson, P. *The History of Mendip Caving.* David & Charles, 1967

CHAPTER 2. NORTH DEVON

Page, J. L. W. *The Coast of Devon and Lundy Island.* Cox, 1895

Harper, C. G. *The North Devon Coast.* Chapman & Hall, 1908

Arber, E. A. N. *The Coast Scenery of North Devon.* Dent, 1911

Burton, S. H. *The North Devon Coast.* Werner Laurie, 1953

Gade, F. W. *Lundy-Bristol Channel*

Etherton, P. T. and Barlow, V. *Lundy—The Tempestuous Isle.* Lutterworth Press, 1960

Archer, C. H. *Coastal Climbs in North Devon.* Privately, 1961

Archer, C. H. *Supplement for 1962.* Privately, 1963

Archer, C. H. *Supplement for 1963-64.* Privately, 1965

Climbers' Club Journal 1960, 1962 and 1964

CHAPTER 3.   EAST AND CENTRAL CORNWALL

Folliott Stokes, A. G. *The Cornish Coast and Moors.* Paul, n.d.

Harper, C. G. *The Cornish Coast (North).* Chapman & Hall, 1910

Harper, C. G. *The Cornish Coast (South).* Chapman & Hall, 1910

Salmon, A. L. *The Cornwall Coast.* Fisher Unwin, 1912

Hockin, J. R. A. *Walking in Cornwall.* Methuen, 1944

Carew, Richard, John Norden's Maps and Ed. by Halliday, F. E. *The Survey of Cornwall.* Melrose, 1953

Burton, S. H. *The Coasts of Cornwall.* Werner Laurie, 1955

Hamilton Jenkin, A. K. *The Cornish Miner.* Allen & Unwin, 1962

Climbers' Club Journal 1960 and 1964

Numerous items from the lists of D. Bradford Barton Ltd, 18 Frances Street, Truro

CHAPTER 4.   WEST PENWITH

Hudson, W. H. *The Land's End.* Hutchinson, 1908

Andrews, A. W. and Pyatt, E. C. *Cornwall.* Climbers' Club, 1950

Banks, M. E. B. *Commando Climber.* Dent, 1955

Vyvyan, C. C. *The Scilly Isles.* Hale, 1960

Kay, E. *Isles of Flowers.* Redman, 1963

Stevenson, V. N. *Cornwall Vol. 2. West and South Coasts of West Penwith.* Climbers' Club, 1966

Biven, P. H. and McDermott, M. B. *Cornwall Vol. 1. North Coast of West Penwith.* Climbers' Club, in the press

Climbers' Club Journal 1905, 1934, 1937, 1938, 1953, etc

Most of references listed for the previous chapter

CHAPTER 5.   SOUTH DEVON

Page, J. L. W. *An Exploration of Dartmoor.* Seeley, 1889

Page, J. L. W. *The Coast of Devon and Lundy Island.* Cox, 1895

Baring Gould, S. *A Book of Dartmoor*. Methuen, 1900
Harper, C. G. *The South Devon Coast*. Chapman & Hall, 1907
Heath, S. *The South Devon and Dorset Coast*. Fisher Unwin, 1910
Derry, J. *Some Rock Climbs near Plymouth*. Privately, 1950
Harvey, L. A. and St Leger Gordon, D. *Dartmoor*. Collins, 1953
Burton, S. II. *The South Devon Coast*. Werner Laurie, 1954
Denton, J. W. *A Climbing Guide to Dartmoor*. Privately, 1954
Ed. by Lawder, K. M. *Climbing Guide to Dartmoor and South West Devon*. Royal Navy Ski & Mountaineering Club, n.d.
Dartmoor National Park Guidebook. H.M.S.O., 1957
Martin, E. W. *Dartmoor*. Hale, 1958
Misuse of a National Park. Dartmoor Preservation Association, 1963
Crossing's Guide to Dartmoor. Reprint by David & Charles, 1965
Shackleton, B. *Interim Guide to the Climbs in the Plymouth Area*. Privately, 1965
Ed. Moulton, R. D. *Rock Climbing in Devonshire*. Royal Navy Ski & Mountaineering Club, 1966
Worth, R. H. *Dartmoor*. Reprinted by David & Charles, 1967
South Devon Climbing Guide. Exeter Climbing Club, in the press
Numerous items from the lists of David & Charles Ltd, Newton Abbot

CHAPTER 6. DORSET

Harper, C. G. *The Dorset Coast*. Chapman & Hall
Heath, S. *The South Devon and Dorset Coast*. Fisher Unwin, 1910
Annette, B. M. *Limestone on the Dorset Coast*. Cade, n.d.
Wightman, R. *Portrait of Dorset*. Hale, 1965
White, R. C. *New Climbs on the Limestone Cliffs of East Dorset*. Southampton University Mountaineering Club, 1967

GLOSSARY

Abseil.   A technique of using the rope for descent. The rope is doubled round a rock spike or through a karabiner *(qv)* in a piton *(qv)* and both ends hang down the rock. There are several different methods of passing the rope round the body, but all include a means of braking and remaining stationary when required. The climber walks down the rocks with his feet against the wall and uses them to control his horizontal direction. Finally the rope can be recovered by pulling on one end.

Arête.   A rock ridge, like a roof ridge, but usually tilted.

Chockstone.   A stone wedged in a cleft in the rock.

Col.   The lowest part of a ridge between two higher points.

Crampons.   A framework of steel spikes attached to the boot sole. Used for the ascent of steep ice, where they eliminate the need for cutting steps with an ice axe.

Étrier.   A rope loop, or a short rope ladder, used for a foothold, usually attached to a piton *(qv)* by means of a karabiner *(qv).*

Gendarme.   A pinnacle or rock mass blocking the route along a ridge, which has to be climbed over or passed by a traverse along its sides.

Karabiner.   A steel snap ring, one side of which can be sprung open so that it can be readily attached to a rope .

Piton. ·An iron spike, usually with a hole at the head, which is hammered into a crack in the rock of suitable width. It can be used either as a belay *ie* to anchor the climber's rope to the rock or for direct aid as a hand or foot hold. In the latter case the hole enables étriers to be attached by means of a karabiner.

Prusik Knots.   A special type of slip knot used for attaching loops of thin rope to the main rope, usually one for each foot and one for behind the shoulders. The knot can be slid up the rope when not under load; when loaded it locks and cannot slip down. The climber is able to ascend a hanging rope therefore by moving the three loops one after the other up the rope, stepping up as necessary from the lower to the higher foot loop.

LIST OF CLUBS AND ORGANISATIONS

National Parks Commission, 1 Cambridge Gate, London, NW1

A government body set up under the National Parks and Access to the Countryside Act, 1949. Administers in the West Country:

(a) National Parks—Dartmoor (365 square miles) and Exmoor (265 square miles).

(b) Areas of Outstanding Natural Beauty—The Quantocks (38 square miles), North Devon Coast (66 square miles), Coasts of Cornwall and Bodmin Moor (together 360 square miles), South Devon Coast (128 square miles), East Devon (103 square miles) and the Coast and part of inland Dorset (400 square miles).

(c) The South-West Peninsula Coast Path.

National Trust, 42 Queen Anne's Gate, London, SW1

A private organisation formed in 1895 and financed by endowments, legacies, donations and subscriptions. Owns approximately 100 square miles of the West Country, including, for example, the coast between Bolt Head and Bolt Tail, Golden Cap, the Cerne Giant, Rough Tor, St Agnes Beacon, Treryn Dinas, Kynance Cove, the Dodman, Glastonbury Tor, Brean Down, etc, etc.

Forestry Commission, 25 Savile Row, London, W1

A government body, founded in 1919, now a very considerable landowner in the country as a whole. A number of their forests are found in the West Country though no one of them is particularly extensive.

Nature Conservancy, 19 Belgrave Square, London, SW1

The government conservation body. Protects numerous West Country sites, including the Axmouth landslip, several caves in the Mendips and in Devon etc, etc.

Royal Society for the Protection of Birds, The Lodge, Sandy, Bedfordshire

A private conservation organisation which administers a number of sites in the West Country, including Steep Holm, etc.

Society for the Promotion of Nature Reserves, British Museum (Natural History), Cromwell Road, London, SW7

The Society owns Nature Reserves and co-ordinates the work of the county naturalists trusts. For the West Country these are the

185

Cornwall Naturalists' Trust, the Devon Trust for Nature Conservation, the Dorset Naturalists' Trust and the Somerset Trust for Nature Conservation.

LOCAL ORGANISATIONS FOR PRESERVATION

(1) Dartmoor Preservation Association, Widecombe-in-the-Moor.
(2) Exmoor Society, Bratton Fleming, Barnstaple.
(3) Lundy Field Society.
(4) Steep Holm Trust.

LOCAL INFORMATION CENTRES

(1) Dartmoor National Park Committee, County Hall, Topsham Road, Exeter.
(2) Dartmoor National Park Information Centre, Two Bridges. (Summer only.)
(3) Exmoor National Park Joint Advisory Committee, County Hall, Taunton, Somerset.
(4) Exmoor National Park Information Centres, Market House, The Parade, Minehead, Somerset and Lyn & Exmoor Museum, Lynton, Devon.

CLIMBING CLUBS WITH A WEST COUNTRY INTEREST

Bristol College of Science and Technology Mountaineering Club, Bristol Exploration Club (Climbing Section), Climbers' Club, Exeter Climbing Club, Gloucestershire Mountaineering Club, Royal Navy Ski & Mountaineering Club, Southampton University Mountaineering Club, University of Bristol Mountaineering Club, Wessex Mountaineering Club.

Current addresses can be obtained from the British Mountaineering Council, 74 South Audley Street, London, W1.

CAVING CLUBS

For the Mendip area—Axbridge Caving Group & Archaeological Society, Bristol Exploration Club, Cave Diving Group, Cave Research Group of Great Britain, Cerberus Speleological Society, Chelsea Speleological Society, Mendip Caving Group, Mendip Nature Research Committee, Royal Military Academy (Sandhurst) Mountaineering & Exploration Society, Shepton Mallet Caving Club, Severn Valley Caving Club, University of Bristol Speleological Society, Wessex Cave Club, Westminster Speleological Group.

For the Devon area—Devon Speleological Society, Pengelly Cave Research Centre, Plymouth Cave Group.

Current addresses can be obtained from the British Speleological Association, Settle, Yorkshire, or from the Central Council for Physical Recreation.

Access to caves on land owned by the Bristol Waterworks Company is controlled by the Charterhouse Caving Committee.

PLACE NAME INDEX

(Four figure National Grid References are given for all features except those which are very extensive, such as large towns, rivers, bays etcetera. The reference gives the co-ordinates of the south west corner of the one kilometre square in which the feature is sited. This simplified co-ordinate system is not unique; every set of four figure co-ordinates is repeated at 100 kilometre intervals both northwards and eastwards, so that the position of a feature must be known within this distance (ie about 60 miles) for the precise location to be found.) References to plates are in bold.

M

Place	Grid ref	page
Hollow Brook Waterfall	6649	56, 65
Holywell Bay	5659	91, 101
Hooe Lake Quarry	4952	158
Hooken Cliff	2287	166
Hope Cove	6739	146
Hope's Nose	9463	150
Horn of Plenty	2009	100, **53**
Horse, The	6713	93, 101
Horseshoe	6449	66
Hotel Buttress	3425	122
Hound Tor	7478/79	155
Hudde Down	6042	92
Hurtstone Point	8949	34
Ilfracombe	—	60, 73
Illiswilgig	8513	131
Irish Lady	3426	122
Izzicumpucca	9109	129
Jamaica Inn	1876	82
Jennifer's Cove	6949	65
Kent's Cavern	9264	159
Kilmar Tor	2574	83, 103
Kimmeridge Bay	9078/79	171
King's Tor Quarry (see Sweltor Quarry)		
Kingswear	8850/51	149
Kipscombe Hill	7649	57
Kit Hill	3771	83
Knaps Longpeak	2018	62, 98
Knight Templar Rock	1346	79
Kynance Cove	6813	93, 101
Ladram Bay	0984/85	166, 179
Lamb Leer	5455	48
Lambert's Castle	36/3798	165
Lametry Bay	1443	77
Lamorna Cove	4524	114
Landewednack	7112	101
Land's End	3425	21, 112-113, 122-123
Lannacombe	8037	148
Lanyon Quoit	4333	109
Leather Tor	5670	154
Lee Bay (Ilfracombe)	4746	60
„ „ (Lynmouth)	6949	58, 64, 66
Levant Mine	3734	112
Lewesdon Hill	4301	28, 165
Lion Rock (Bude)	2007	100
„ „ (Kynance)	6812	93
Litter Water	2016	56, 85

GENERAL AND PERSONAL INDEX